BARACK OBAMA

The Making of a President

by Dawne Allette

Tamarind

BARACK OBAMA: THE MAKING OF A PRESIDENT
A TAMARIND BOOK 978 1 848 53022 5

First published in Great Britain by Tamarind Books,
a division of Random House Children's Books
A Random House Group Company

Tamarind Books edition published 2009

1 3 5 7 9 10 8 6 4 2

The Random House Group Limited supports the Forest Stewardship Council (FSC),
the leading international forest certification organization. All our titles that are
printed on Greenpeace-approved FSC-certified paper carry the FSC logo. Our paper
procurement policy can be found at www.rbooks.co.uk/environment.

Set in Humanist

Tamarind Books are published by Random House Children's Books,
61–63 Uxbridge Road, London W5 5SA

www.**tamarindbooks**.co.uk
www.**kids**at**randomhouse**.co.uk
www.**rbooks**.co.uk

Addresses for companies within The Random House Group Limited can be found
at: www.randomhouse.co.uk/offices.htm

THE RANDOM HOUSE GROUP Limited Reg. No. 954009

A CIP catalogue record for this book is available from the British Library.

Printed and bound in Great Britain by
CPI Bookmarque, Croydon, CR0 4TD

For Tsekani and Yohance

and

Special thanks to Mark Reutter
for his support and encouragement

Barack Obama has links to many parts of the world. Here are some of the key countries – and places in the USA – that feature in his life.

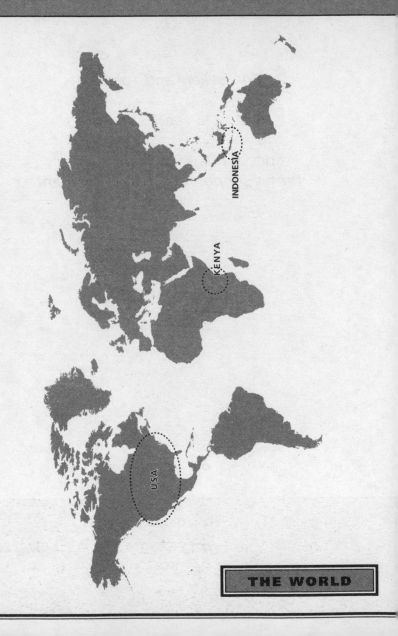

INDONESIA

KENYA

USA

THE WORLD

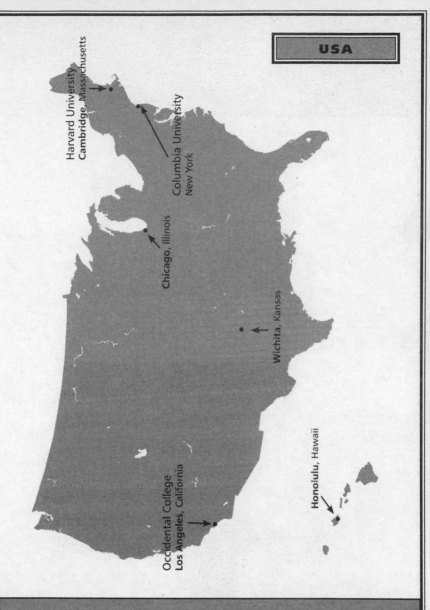

USA

Harvard University
Cambridge, Massachusetts

Columbia University
New York

Chicago, Illinois

Wichita, Kansas

Occidental College
Los Angeles, California

Honolulu, Hawaii

*'As the world grows smaller, our
common humanity shall reveal itself.'*
Barack Obama, January 2009,
in his Inaugural address

PROLOGUE

'No dream is beyond our grasp if we reach for it, and fight for it and work for it . . .'

The thunderous applause, mingled with loud music, sounded like a rock concert or a Premiership football match. But this was not a concert or sporting event. This was a political event. More than 80,000 Americans had descended on Denver, Colorado, USA, to see and hear Barack Obama. In an electrifying speech, he accepted the Democratic Party's nomination for President of the United States. He was the first African American to become the nominee of a major political party. Some

1

people cried with joy. Over and above the deafening noise, three words came loud and clear, over and over:

'YES WE CAN, YES WE CAN!'

The next stage was the competition for the actual job of President. In the previous months, all the candidates for the nomination had covered thousands of miles, travelling across America, campaigning to win the chance to go for one of the world's most powerful jobs. Never in the history of the United States of America had a black person been elected as President.

Now the two nominees – one for the Republican Party, John McCain, and one for the Democratic Party, Barack Obama – began the final race to the top.

Barack Obama won. He received over 52% of the popular vote to defeat his opponent, whose Republican Party had controlled the presidency since 2001. Never before in the history of American politics was there such overwhelming multi-racial support for a presidential candidate.

On 20 January 2009, Barack Obama was sworn in as the 44th President of the United States, in Washington, DC.

His amazing story is one of dedication and determination. His father was a Kenyan African and his mother a white American. Obama's life is an example of overcoming incredible odds. All over the world, many children have shared his early life experiences: a child whose father left the family home and whose single mother struggled to do the job of two parents.

In one campaign speech he said: 'I was not born into money or status. I was born to a teenage mom in Hawaii, and my dad left us when I was two. But my family gave me love, they gave me education, and most of all they gave me hope – hope that in America no dream is beyond our grasp if we reach for it, and fight for it and work for it.'

As a young man, Barack Obama underwent periods of doubt and confusion. After university, he became a community organizer in a poor neighbourhood in Chicago. He could have gone off the rails, and at one stage in his life he was heading that way, but today he is the most important man in America, and has great influence in countries all over the world.

He is a devoted husband and father. His smart and resourceful wife, Michelle, a successful lawyer, was closely involved in his campaign for the presidency. He has two daughters, Malia and Sasha. The Obama family now live in Washington, DC in the presidential mansion, the White House.

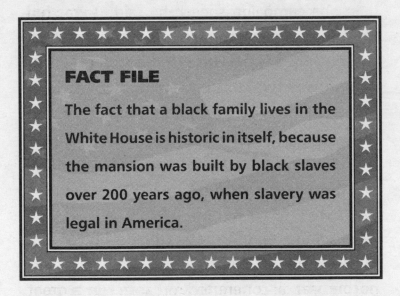

FACT FILE

The fact that a black family lives in the White House is historic in itself, because the mansion was built by black slaves over 200 years ago, when slavery was legal in America.

Many black heroes and heroines forced America to change its laws and social attitudes towards African Americans.

These pioneers helped in the struggle against oppression, and their efforts went a long way to make Barack Obama's journey to the White House possible. One such pioneer was Rosa Parks in 1955. Back then, black passengers travelling by bus were made to sit at the back or leave the bus if a white person needed space. Rosa Parks refused to give up her seat on a city bus to a white male passenger and was arrested and imprisoned for doing so. Later, Martin Luther King, who spoke powerfully of his dream for equality in America, led a grassroots movement that demanded equal rights for black people. He was shot and killed in 1968.

When Barack Obama took the steps that led to the White House, he acknowledged his debt to these heroes:

'I think it is fair to say were it not for that quiet moment of courage by Mrs Parks, I would not be standing here today. I owe her a great thanks, as does the nation.'

FACT FILE

Martin Luther King (1929–1968) was born in Georgia. A strong advocate of non-violent action, he became one of the most noted leaders of the American civil rights movement. In August 1963, he participated in a huge civil rights march on Washington and gave his famous 'I Have a Dream' speech, in which he spoke of his hope for freedom and equality for all in America. In 1964 he was awarded the Nobel Peace Prize. He was shot and killed by James Earl Ray in April 1968. Dr King was just 39 years old.

CHAPTER ONE

'I was not born into money or status. I was born to a teenage mom in Hawaii, and my dad left us when I was two . . .'

Barack Obama was twenty-one years old when he received the terrible news that his father was dead. He had been killed in a car accident, thousands of miles away in Kenya. Barack sat in his small, rundown New York apartment and tried to measure his loss.

His father had left him and his mother in 1963, when Barack was just two years old. Now Barack sat alone and tried to visualize his father. He remembered the stories he had heard from his mother, his grandmother and grandfather – stories about a witty, scholarly and intelligent man called Barack Onyango Obama. He thought about what he had learned. They had never criticized him. Although his mother might have been upset over the failed marriage, she never spoke ill of him.

His father, after whom he was named, was born in 1936 in Kenya, East Africa. He was a member of the Luo people and lived in a village called Alego, near Lake Victoria. As a student in Kenya, Barack Senior was mischievous and was often in trouble. He was not fond of school and played truant for long periods of time. However, he always turned up for examinations at the end of term and did very well. He was an extremely intelligent young man.

After gaining admission to the prestigious Maseno School in Kenya, he was expelled for getting into trouble and for missing classes. This caused his parents to worry that their son would never achieve anything. They dispatched him to Mombasa, the capital city, where he

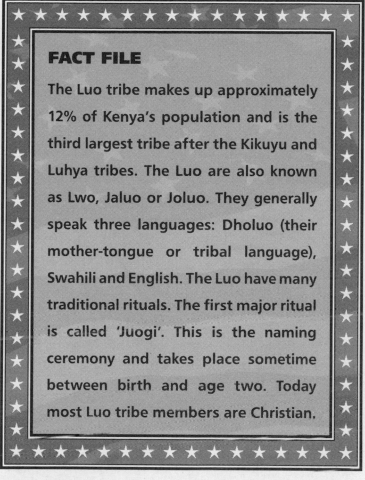

found work as a clerk. It was there that he met and married his first wife, Kezia. They had a son, Roy.

In order to find a better job to support his family, Barack Senior needed to get into further education. He signed up for a correspondence course which would qualify him to attend university in the United States. He did well, but actually going to university was expensive and he had little money. He applied for a scholarship and was accepted by the University of Hawaii.

He left Kenya and travelled to America alone. It was 1959.

Barack Senior was the first and only African student on the campus. He studied econometrics, which is the study of solving problems in the economy using mathematics. He was a brilliant and disciplined student and graduated at the top of his class, completing a four-year programme in just three years.

It was at the University of Hawaii that he met Stanley Ann Dunham. She was a shy eighteen-year-old student. He was twenty-three. They were taking a Russian language class together and became attracted to each other.

Barack Sr was tall and skinny with a bright smile and a rich, deep voice. Stanley Ann was quiet. She was petite with dark curly hair and brown eyes. She was born in Kansas, a farming state in the Midwest of America, and was the daughter of furniture store manager Stanley and his wife, Madelyn.

The name Stanley had been given to her by her father, whose name was also Stanley. He had wanted a son, so he named her Stanley Ann.

She was studying at the university and had moved with her parents to Hawaii from a small town near Seattle, Washington.

Even as a very young girl, Ann was aware that racism existed in many parts of America. There were deep divisions between blacks and whites. One day, she was playing with a friend under a tree outside her home. Her friend was a black girl. A group of white children saw them together and shouted very nasty names at them. Just in time, Ann's mother arrived and told the girls to get into the house for safety. The frightened friend ran off along the road at great speed, too terrified to go into the house. The next day, Ann's father reported the incident to the head teacher of the school. But all the teachers and parents said the same thing: that white girls in their town didn't play with black girls.

Ann was an only child and she suffered from asthma. Her family moved house often, looking for the right place to live. Because of this she spent a great deal of time on her own, reading. This was her favourite pastime. When she turned eighteen, she applied and was accepted at a university in Chicago, but her father thought that she was much too young to live on campus on her own. When he found a job as a furniture salesman in Hawaii, they all moved there and Ann attended the University of Hawaii. It was here that she met Barack Obama Sr.

The two young people spent a great deal of time together. Since they were both keen students, they had lively discussions and enjoyed each other's company immensely. Then they fell in love.

One evening, Ann invited Barack to have dinner with her parents. They found him charming and intelligent, with excellent manners. Despite this, her parents were

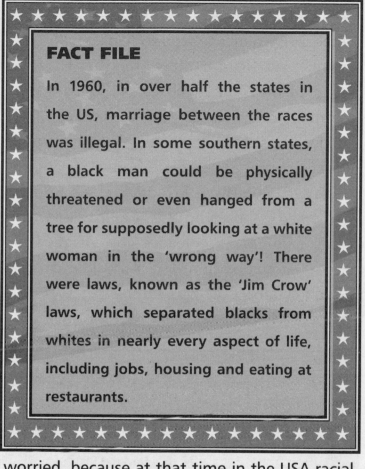

worried, because at that time in the USA racial prejudice was rife.

The young couple made plans to be married, even though this was not an easy decision for them. But Ann, besides being an exceptional student, was an independent thinker and did not allow the prejudices of other people to determine whom she would marry.

Ann and Barack flew to the Hawaiian island of Maui on 2 February 1961 and were married in a small civil ceremony. They believed that they could make their marriage work.

On 4 August 1961, Ann and Barack welcomed a son into the world. He was a healthy, robust little fellow and weighed 8lb 2oz. They named him Barack Hussein Obama, after his father. He was nicknamed Barry. He was a lively, loveable child.

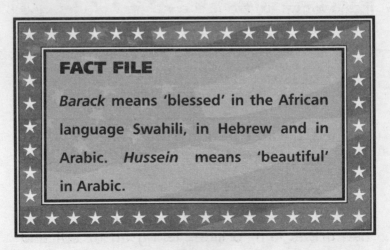

FACT FILE

Barack means 'blessed' in the African language Swahili, in Hebrew and in Arabic. *Hussein* means 'beautiful' in Arabic.

After Barack was born, his father, an ambitious man, continued his studies and was granted another scholarship, this time to Harvard, a highly prestigious university in Massachusetts on the east coast of the USA, 5,000 miles away. He was to study for his PhD in economics. He accepted the offer because a degree from Harvard would equip him for leadership back in Kenya, his homeland. This was his dream. However, the offer of a place at Harvard did not allow enough money to support the whole family. When he was offered a scholarship from another university, which would allow him to bring his family along, he still chose to enrol at Harvard. He went alone. The couple decided that at the completion of his studies, Ann and young Barack would join him, and together they would move back to Africa.

Ann stayed on in Hawaii and took care of her son with support from her parents. But when she learned of her husband's first wife and family in Kenya and considered how his ambition had driven him to live apart from herself and their child, she filed for divorce. It was 1964.

CHAPTER TWO

'I know what it means to have an absent father . . .'

Barry continued to live in Hawaii with his mother and grandparents when his father returned to Kenya. He called his grandfather Gramps. The Hawaiian word for grandmother is *tutu*. Young Barry called her 'Toot'.

Hawaii is an archipelago, or chain of islands, located in the Pacific Ocean about midway between America and Japan. The most populated island is Oahu, which is also the location of Hawaii's largest city, Honolulu. There are tropical rain forests, spectacular sunsets and broad expanses of white sandy beaches. The islands grow a large selection of flowers and fruits, including papaya, mangoes, guava and tamarind. Large shoals of fish populate the surrounding seas.

Despite all its beauty, Hawaii has its own troubled past. The first settlers were sea-migrating Polynesians from islands near Australia, who had rowed their canoes across thousands of miles of open sea to reach the islands. They developed elaborate societies headed by powerful chiefs and priests.

The English explorer Captain James Cook made the first European discovery of Hawaii in 1778. He was killed a year later during a confrontation with natives after he tried to take the Hawaiian king hostage. Christian missionaries soon arrived and brought churches and horse-drawn vehicles. American settlers moved in and set up huge plantations in the rich volcanic soil. They grew pineapples, sugarcane and many tropical fruits. The native population dwindled as they had no immunity to the diseases brought to the islands by these settlers. Filipino, Japanese and Chinese people were taken in and they formed the new work force.

Hawaii became a US territory in 1900. In 1959 it became the 50th and final American state.

In this vibrant, multicultural setting, young Barack Obama spent his early years.

His father was not involved in his life and Gramps became a father figure for little Barry.

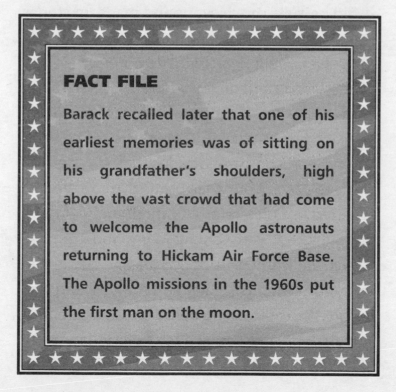

FACT FILE

Barack recalled later that one of his earliest memories was of sitting on his grandfather's shoulders, high above the vast crowd that had come to welcome the Apollo astronauts returning to Hickam Air Force Base. The Apollo missions in the 1960s put the first man on the moon.

His mother and both grandparents shared stories with him about his father and their time spent with him. These stories conjured up positive images in his mind and the many family photographs provided visual images of his absent father.

Since the black population in Hawaii was small, tourists to the island would sometimes stare at little Barry and ask who he was. Gramps could be quite mischievous and made up stories that Barry was the great-grandson of a Hawaiian king. He would roar with laughter when the tourists took out their cameras excitedly and shot picture after picture of his grandson, thinking he was royalty. When he wasn't poking fun at the tourists, Gramps did his best to protect Barry from the insensitivity of people who did not understand his heritage.

As a child, Barry spent many hours on the beach. He learned to body surf and he was an excellent swimmer. Early some mornings, well before the roosters crowed, he would scramble out of bed and set off for Kailua Bay. Barry watched the men dive into the still, black water with their flashlights and then emerge with big shiny fish at the end of their spears. The fish were called humu-humu-nuku-nuku-apua, or 'trigger fish with a pig-like short snout', translated into English. A tasty mouthful of fish that matched the mouthful of words for its name.

CHAPTER THREE

'Our patchwork heritage is a strength, not a weakness . . . as the world grows smaller, our common humanity shall reveal itself . . .'

After her divorce from Barry's father in 1964, Ann returned to her studies at the University of Hawaii. Here she met an Indonesian student by the name of Lolo Soetero. Lolo means 'crazy' in Hawaii, and this name caused Gramps to shake with laughter many times. Lolo, however, was nothing like his name suggested. He was a well-mannered man with a quiet temperament. He spent many hours patiently playing chess with Gramps.

Like Hawaii, Indonesia – Lolo's homeland – is an archipelago of islands, but it is vastly larger. The country consists of 13,000 islands, of which only about 1,000 are inhabited. The islands are located in Asia, between the Pacific and Indian oceans.

Indonesia is a country with a turbulent history. It is the largest nation in Southeast Asia. For many years, it was ruled by the Netherlands and was called the Dutch East Indies. To gain its independence, there was a fierce and bloody struggle between the native Indonesians and Dutch colonialists. Many lives were lost, including Lolo's father and brother who died when the Dutch army burned down their home. Independence from Dutch rule eventually came in 1945. There was a new Indonesian government with a new president. However, the people eventually became unhappy with the government and conflict erupted. Young Indonesians studying abroad were ordered to return to Indonesia to join the army, and in 1966 Lolo was called up.

By then Ann and Lolo had fallen in love and

they decided to marry. Lolo returned home. He found a home for them and, early in 1967, Ann and Barry flew to Indonesia. Barry was six years old.

This place was very different from Hawaii. When they arrived at their new home, Barry must have thought that they owned a zoo. Spectacular coloured and plumed birds perched in the trees high above the garden, while on the ground, there were squawking chickens, quacking ducks, a yellow dog and a couple of baby crocodiles.

Lolo bought his stepson a young gibbon as a welcoming present. A gibbon is a small ape that lives in trees and moves faster than any other land mammal.

FACT FILE

Barry's pet gibbon in Indonesia was named Tata.

Barry was unsure about this new pet at first – he thought it was a monkey – but the pair would eventually become best friends.

Barry's first dinner in Indonesia was memorable. He watched in shocked silence as Lolo killed the main course for the meal, a plump chicken. He sliced the bird's neck clean through with a sharp knife. He then tossed the headless creature up in the air and let it fall to the ground, where it flapped about for a short time and then stopped moving. The chicken proved to be very tasty when stewed with deliciously flavoured spices on a bed of rice.

Gradually Ann, Lolo and Barry settled down to life together. Ann found a job teaching English to Indonesian businessmen, Lolo began work as a geologist for the Indonesian army and Barry began making friends with the local children. They lived in a comfortable house, but all around them the houses were built from bamboo. There was poverty everywhere.

Lolo made sure that Barry learned the Indonesian language, and it was not long before he was fluent. Lolo explained the country's customs so that Barry knew what to expect and how to cope with his new life. He regularly played on the streets, so Lolo bought him a pair of boxing gloves so that he could defend himself if he needed to. Most of the time, though, the youngsters played well together, catching crickets, doing odd jobs and flying kites. Barry shared many things with them, including chicken pox and measles!

Indonesia was one of the world's poorest countries, with many families earning less than £100 a year. Barry felt sorry for the beggars on the streets. Some of them had no arms. Others walked on their hands because they had no feet. His mother made sure that he was kind to people who were less fortunate than he was. One day, for instance, when they saw yet another homeless person, she asked him to imagine how he would feel if he were standing in that person's shoes.

Lolo, however, did not see the point of trying to give money to every beggar. He told Barry that since he only had a little money himself, if he were to start giving it away, he would end up with nothing just like the beggars.

Ann and Lolo could not afford to send Barry to the International School for foreigners in Jakarta. He attended two different schools, a Catholic grammar school and later a state school.

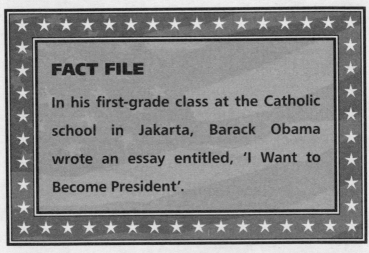

FACT FILE

In his first-grade class at the Catholic school in Jakarta, Barack Obama wrote an essay entitled, 'I Want to Become President'.

In Indonesia, Barry stood out from the children around him. In Hawaii, there were many children of various ethnic groups. Here, his peer group was much shorter and slimmer, quite different from the tall, dark, curly-haired Barry. His classmates gave him the nickname 'Curly Eyelashes' because his eyelashes were not as straight as theirs.

He was remembered by a teacher as being 'very smart in mathematics'. He was also very disciplined because of his mother's influence. She was concerned about his education and sometimes woke him up at 4.30 in the morning so that he could prepare for his lessons for that school day and practise his English. Ann sent off for a correspondence course for her son, much like the ones his father had taken many years ago in Kenya.

When Barry was nine years old, his sister Maya was born. Indonesia was now in political turmoil following the seizure of power by the military. Worried about his safety and his education under these conditions, Ann decided to send Barry back to Honolulu to live with Gramps and Toot and attend an American school.

CHAPTER FOUR

'I have brothers, sisters, nieces, nephews, uncles, and cousins of every race and hue scattered across three continents . . .'

Barry was ten years old when he returned to Hawaii. His grandfather was now selling insurance and his grandmother worked at a bank where she became the first female vice president. Gramps and Toot moved from their house to a two-bedroom apartment near Barry's new school.

His grandparents enrolled him at the prestigious Punahou private school. It was founded in 1841 and had a reputation for academic excellence. The school building sat in several acres of land. The classrooms were large and airy, and there were tennis courts and swimming pools. On the first day of school, Gramps accompanied Barry across the lush campus grounds to Room 307 in Castle Hall, which was Miss Hefty's classroom.

Starting at the new school was a difficult experience for a young boy with an unusual name, dark complexion and curly hair. The other children were mostly rich and white. They had grown up together and were used to each other.

They were curious about him and kept trying to touch his hair. They teased him about his father being an African. One boy even asked Barry if his father ate people! This brought hoots of laughter from the other children. This was a false stereotype that some people still had about African people being cannibals. When Miss Hefty learned that Barack's father was from Kenya, she asked him which tribe he belonged to. Barry answered quietly, 'Luo'. For some reason, the children found this very funny and began misbehaving. They laughed loudly and made monkey sounds. It was a very embarrassing experience. Barry's first day of school was awful and he was glad when it was finally over.

Although his classmates teased him relentlessly, they were not cruel. They didn't beat him up or pick fights with him. After a while they simply lost interest in making fun of him. The novelty of having him in the class had quickly worn off.

At first Barry thought that he would never fit in with kids who didn't wear sandals like his playmates in Jakarta and who rode skateboards and played American football rather than soccer and badminton. He became a good surfer and soccer player, but loved basketball best of all. After his initial reservation about skateboarding, he became fairly good at that too.

As they got to know and understand him better, the children teased him less and less. In spite of this, Barry still felt left out and alone and sought out the so-called misfits at the school. These included girls who thought they were too tall or shy, boys who always misbehaved, and kids with asthma who were considered sickly.

Barry's love of reading comic books started at this time. He especially enjoyed the adventures of Spider-Man and Conan the Barbarian and any superheroes with unusual powers. Collecting comic books became a lifelong hobby. Among his other historic firsts, Barack Obama is believed to be the first US President to bring a collection of 'Spidey' comics to the White House.

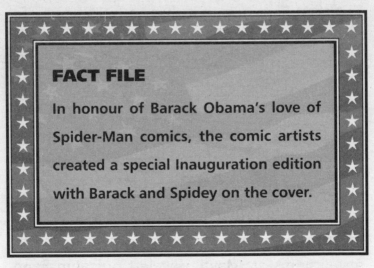

FACT FILE

In honour of Barack Obama's love of Spider-Man comics, the comic artists created a special Inauguration edition with Barack and Spidey on the cover.

CHAPTER FIVE

'My mother was born in the heartland of America, but my father grew up herding goats in Kenya. His father – my grandfather – was a cook, a domestic servant to the British . . .'

One day in 1971, the year Barry returned to Honolulu, Toot received an important telegram from Kenya. It was from Barry's father. He was coming to visit for the Christmas holidays. He had survived a terrible car accident and was recuperating from his injuries. Barry's mother and little sister, Maya, were also coming from Indonesia at the same time. His mother's marriage to Lolo had ended and she was returning to Hawaii with Maya.

Barry had not seen his father since he was two years old. His mother had stayed in touch with him by letter and as Barry grew older, Ann had always kept him up to date with news of his father and stories about Kenya. She told Barry about his nomadic Luo tribe and how they had migrated to Kenya from their original home along a great river. She spoke to him about Jomo Kenyatta, the President of Kenya, and told him that the President's name meant 'burning spear'. She also told him that his father had remarried, and that Barry now had five sisters and one brother living in Kenya. Barry, in the meantime, was telling his classmates that his grandfather was the chief of his African tribe and that his father, whose name meant 'burning spear', would take over when his grandfather died.

'What will happen after that?' one boy asked.

Barry explained that he probably would have to become the tribal chief, but cautioned that his father was obliged to settle all of the fighting for power before his son went back to Kenya. His classmates were very impressed to hear that there might be a prince among them and started including him more in their games and activities.

On the day of his father's arrival, Miss Hefty, his class teacher, let Barry go home early. When he arrived home, he stood outside the door hesitantly. His heart was thumping wildly. When he was finally brave enough to walk into the house, he was shocked by what he saw. From the stories Barry had been told by Gramps and his mother, he had expected to meet a proud, strong, tall man. What he saw was a skinny man who walked with a limp. Behind his horn-rimmed glasses, his eyes were yellowed and he did not appear to be at all healthy. He was, however, smartly dressed in a blue jacket, white shirt and a scarlet necktie. Could this possibly be the same man that Gramps said had the strength of a god?

Before Barack Sr went to bed that evening, he pressed three things into his son's hands. They were wooden figurines: one of an elephant, another of a lion and the last of an ebony man in a tribal outfit beating a drum.

His father told Barry they were only small gifts. Barry thanked his father for these presents from Kenya.

Barry felt uncomfortable in the presence of his father. One night when Barry wanted to watch the movie *How the Grinch Stole Christmas* by Dr Seuss, his father made him turn off the television. He told him he needed to pay more attention to his studies. This caused an argument among the adults. Barry's father claimed that they were spoiling him. Barry did not feel that his father had earned the right to suddenly come into his life and try to discipline him.

But he soon noticed other things about his father. He noticed that when he spoke, everyone in the family, including his mother, was energized. They hung onto his every word as he spoke of politics and Africa. Even Toot, who seldom gave an opinion, would leave whatever she was doing to join in the discussion.

When his father talked about racism in America, he was optimistic for the future. He made it seem as though Martin Luther King had never been shot and killed by a white supremacist while fighting for the equality of blacks in America, that racist laws were only temporary setbacks, and that, in the words of former US President Franklin Roosevelt, 'the only thing we have to fear is fear itself'. Barry began to feel that his father had a strange power and felt that he might even become a permanent presence in his life.

Then after a couple of days, his mother informed him that Miss Hefty, his teacher at Punahou School, had invited his father to speak to his class.

Barry panicked. He recalled the tall tales he had told his classmates about his father's royal status. He wished that these stories were true. He was afraid that the children would laugh at his father the way they had laughed at him. How would his classmates react to his father's stories? How was he going to explain that he wasn't in line to become an African prince? These and other questions lashed through his head like thunderbolts in a raging storm.

Then the visit happened. Miss Hefty

introduced Barry's father to the class, telling them how he had come all the way from Kenya, in Africa, and that he would tell them about his country.

Barack Sr spoke of the wild animals in Kenya that still roamed on the plains. He explained that in some tribes a young boy still had to kill a lion to prove his manhood. He talked about the Luos and how they sat under trees in a group to create laws for the tribe. He recounted how many of his people were oppressed because of the colour of their skin, how they fought to be free from colonialism, and how the children of Kenya wanted to improve their lives and develop their skills like everyone else in the world.

The children and the teachers listened, wide-eyed. They were impressed with Barack Sr's intelligence and the stories he told. They applauded loudly when he was done.

Barry's father had impressed everyone and both his teachers and his classmates told Barry so – even the boy who had once asked him whether his father ate people.

Barack as a baby
with his mother,
Stanley Ann Dunham

Barack Onyango Obama,
Barack Obama's father

Barack with Gramps – playing in the surf in Hawaii

Above: In Indonesia, with his stepfather Lolo Soetoro, his mother and baby half-sister Maya

Below: Barack (circled) with his class at school in Jakarta

Barack's father was a 'hit' when he came to Hawaii

Graduation – an important step on Barack's path to success

. . . but Barack also loves his sports!

Gramps and Toot visiting New York,
where Barack is studying politics

Barack meets his relatives in Kenya – including Granny Sarah Onyango (**above**) and his sister Auma (front left, **below**)

Retracing his father's footsteps by studying at Harvard University

Barry's father was a hit. He had lived up to his reputation of being a great man.

After that, Barry wanted to be with his father as much as he could. They went to concerts and visited his dad's old school friends. Basketball became even more important to Barry after his father bought him a basketball for Christmas.

One day his dad played a record he had brought with him from Africa on Gramps' old stereo. He grabbed his son playfully and invited him to learn from 'the master'. Barry and his dad danced around the room holding onto each other and laughing. Ann smiled and Gramps and Toot looked on as the two swayed to the haunting tune. In the middle of a Hawaiian afternoon Barry was learning to dance like a Luo to the African rhythm.

The next day his father was gone.

CHAPTER SIX

'When I was a young man, I thought life was all about me – how do I make my way in the world, and how do I become successful . . .'

The summer after his father's visit, Toot took Barry, his mother and Maya on a tour of mainland America. Among the places they visited were Washington and California, where they went to Disneyland and also visited Yellowstone Park. It was Barry's first trip to the American mainland.

Ann stayed in Hawaii and returned to graduate school. She looked after Barry and Maya until Barry was thirteen years old. They had fun together, often going hiking and on great

43

picnics. Although she was now separated from Lolo, Ann decided to return to Indonesia to complete her studies in anthropology, the study of human development throughout history.

She had planned to take both children with her, but Barry decided against going. He told his mother that he did not want to experience what it was like to be new and different yet again. Ann understood that he had managed to cope with the new life in Indonesia and then another big readjustment to Hawaii, so she accepted his decision. She and Maya left, and Barry settled in with his grandparents.

One reason Barry decided to stay was because he wanted to learn who he truly was. He needed to know what it was really like to be a black man in America. He had read a magazine article about a black man who had tried to peel off his skin because he wanted so much to be white. The story haunted Barry. He knew that his appearance defined him as a black man in America, but beyond that, it seemed that no one really knew exactly what that meant – what kind of man he should aspire to be.

He wanted to be like his father, but his father was absent and provided few clues as to how he should conduct himself. His advice was that Barry would eventually find himself drawn to the right career – but this wasn't clear enough to help guide Barry through the doubts and complexities of his teenage years.

With many confusing thoughts going around in his head, he directed his energy into improving his basketball game. He spent hour after hour, sometimes well into the night, on a court near his home. Toot stood and watched him from the apartment window as he bounced and dribbled and shot basket after basket, first with two hands and then with one. He had style.

With the help of some older kids, he learned to cock the ball behind his left ear and then shot-put it towards the rim. His speciality move was a left-hand shot from the corner of the court, placing a little backspin on the ball and launching it with a low arc. On the basketball court, Barry found that skin colour didn't matter. Being black was no disadvantage. He played with both white and black kids and established some of his closest friendships there. The game gave him confidence in himself.

Gramps also took Barry to a University of Hawaii game. Years later, Barry wrote with star-struck enthusiasm about watching the team warm up. He remembered how, to him, the players had seemed more like warriors than boys – confident, powerful and at ease in their roles. They had winked at the girls and casually demonstrated a few skilled moves before the game itself had begun. And then it had been like a battle they were determined to win.

The university team back in 1971–72 had won 23 games and lost only 5. They played on the strength of their five black starters, known as 'The Fabulous Five'.

Barry joined the Punahou School basketball team in the 10th grade. His coach was nicknamed 'Mr Fundamentals' and frowned at the behind-the-back passes and fancy spin moves that Barack had picked up on the asphalt courts near his home. Barry and the coach had several disputes. During his three years on the team,

Barry was never in the starting lineup. Despite these frustrations, he enjoyed practising with the team and got in enough playing time to win recognition for his excellent jump shot, which became known as the 'Barry O'Bomber'. During the team's state championship win in his senior year, Barry scored two points.

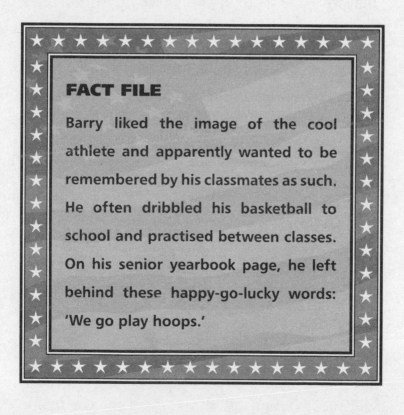

FACT FILE

Barry liked the image of the cool athlete and apparently wanted to be remembered by his classmates as such. He often dribbled his basketball to school and practised between classes. On his senior yearbook page, he left behind these happy-go-lucky words: 'We go play hoops.'

CHAPTER SEVEN

'Growing up, I absorbed a lot of negative stereotypes about how I should behave as a black teenager and fell into some of the same traps that a lot of black male youth do . . .'

There was another side to Barry that he kept hidden from his classmates.

He was searching for his identity.

He was aware that he was an American with African ancestry. His mother had always told him what a remarkable man his father was. She encouraged Barry to be like him, but he didn't know his father. The one visit when Barry was ten years old had been brief. His father did write to him and Barry replied, but he wasn't as close to his father as he was to his mother, Gramps and Toot. He had never met any of his African relatives. He was a troubled young man, searching for answers.

Off the basketball court, he observed interactions between whites and blacks that disturbed him. Sometimes it involved his black friends, who would 'diss' or criticize white people. Barry occasionally became involved in their grievances, only to remember that Gramps, Toot and his mother – all white people – loved him. Sometimes he'd get into fights and use the skills that Lolo had taught him to survive on the streets of Indonesia. Once he gave a boy a bloody nose for calling him a 'coon' – a derogatory word for a black person.

Even his grandmother was not immune. Overhearing a row between his grandparents one night, Barry asked Gramps what the problem was. He explained that Toot had made a totally unnecessary fuss when she was bothered in the street by a beggar. Gramps thought that this was because the beggar was black.

Barry needed someone outside the family with whom he could discuss his confusion.

Gramps had a close friend, a black poet named Frank Marshall Davis, who listened sympathetically to Barry's concerns. Frank was 80 years old and had lived through many hardships caused by racial inequality.

Frank explained to Barry that even though his grandparents were good people they could not truly understand the experience of a black man in America. In their early years, they had grown up in a world where, if Frank happened to meet them walking along a pavement, Frank would have had to step off the kerb to let them pass. In those days, blacks had to understand – even defer to – white people in order to survive, Frank told Barry. White people, on the other hand, did not have to understand, or even recognize, black people if they chose not to.

Barry had used basketball not only as a sport, but also as a means of escape from the pain he was feeling. He started smoking cigarettes and then drifted into experimenting with drugs and alcohol. As a result, his grades began to slip.

All around him, he saw trouble, especially among the kids who didn't go to the privileged

Punahou School. Several lost their lives in drunken car crashes. Others went to prison on drug charges. He felt a sense of powerlessness and hopelessness and, as he admitted later, he used drugs as an escape – a way of avoiding facing up to the issues he needed to address: who he was, and who he wanted to be.

His confusion and distress were expressed indirectly in a poem that he submitted to the school literary magazine:

'An old, forgotten man
on an old, forgotten road,
who walks a straight line
along the crooked world.'

When his mother returned to Hawaii after completing her studies in Indonesia, Barry was in his senior year of high school and ready for graduation.

Ann knew something was wrong with her son. She expressed her disappointment with his attitude and his mediocre grades. She confronted him about his poor choices and said that she did not raise a child, especially a child as bright as he was, who was content with just

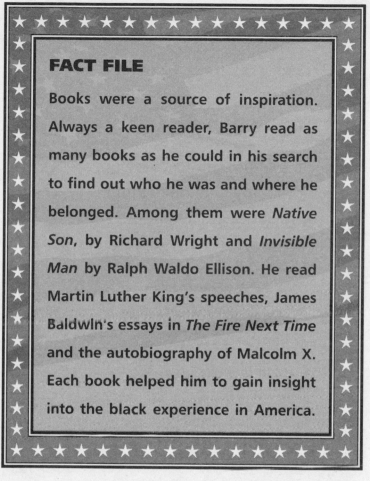

FACT FILE

Books were a source of inspiration. Always a keen reader, Barry read as many books as he could in his search to find out who he was and where he belonged. Among them were *Native Son*, by Richard Wright and *Invisible Man* by Ralph Waldo Ellison. He read Martin Luther King's speeches, James Baldwin's essays in *The Fire Next Time* and the autobiography of Malcolm X. Each book helped him to gain insight into the black experience in America.

getting by in life. Barry responded defiantly, saying that it was no big deal and that he might 'goof off' and stay in Hawaii and attend college on a part-time basis. He told his mother that life was just one big game of chance anyway – what was the point of it all? He had not sent out any college applications.

Ann was angry. She remembered that she too had rebelled against her parents by ignoring their advice and marrying a man she did not know as well as she thought she did. Now she told her son to shape up, saying that he could do anything he wanted if he put his mind to it. She wanted him to understand that his future was in his own hands – he couldn't just expect luck to see him through.

They had many serious discussions and arguments about his future. Finally it was decided that he would attend Occidental College, a small liberal arts school, in an effort to turn his life around.

CHAPTER EIGHT

'The dream we share is more powerful than the differences we have . . .'

Barry Obama started Occidental College in 1979, with a full scholarship and a vow to make a fresh start. Occidental College in California – on the west coast of the USA – had a large campus set in idyllic surroundings. Hanging out with basketball players no longer interested Barry, and he made a point of staying away from the druggies.

He also remembered what Gramps' friend Frank Davis had said to him about university education – his belief that college sometimes trained black people to give up their own heritage and do what white people wanted. He warned Barry to be aware of how easily this could happen.

Occidental College had a very diverse student body and Barry chose his friends carefully. He was attracted to the so-called 'campus radicals'. They included politically motivated black students, performance poets and foreign students. In this group, Barry enjoyed wide-ranging debates about life in a variety of cultures.

One of Barry's favourite professors was Roger Boesche. In Boesche's classroom he learned about the world, and that it did not revolve around him. He was becoming less self-centred. The course was on modern political thought, and Barry's teacher played an instrumental role in pushing him to excel in his studies.

In 1980, when Barry was in his sophomore or second year, he and his friends became involved in a political cause. They were learning about apartheid in South Africa. They were disturbed to hear that white settlers from the Netherlands and Britain had moved to South Africa many years before and now held all the power in the country.

FACT FILE

Nelson Mandela is a qualified lawyer and ex-President of South Africa. But living under apartheid, he could never have aimed for freedom and success. Mandela worked at a law firm providing free or low-cost help to many blacks who were unfairly treated by the apartheid government. Obama would later do similar legal work. Mandela opposed the racist system through political activity. He became a key leader of the African National Congress Party. When police shot dead several peaceful black protesters, Mandela's group felt unable to challenge the system without using force. In 1964 he was given a lifelong prison sentence. He was allowed to receive only two visitors and two letters a year. During these years of solitude he studied for another law degree. In 1990, after 27 years, at the age of 72, he was freed and in 1994 Mandela became President of South Africa in the country's first fully representative democratic election. He has received international respect and recognition, including the Nobel Peace Prize in 1993. There is a statue of Nelson Mandela in London's Parliament Square.

Apartheid was a system of racial segregation that excluded the native Africans from well-paid jobs, education, housing and medical care. A minority of whites in South Africa controlled most of the country's wealth, while blacks were forced into a life of servitude and uncertainty. This was what it had been like in America under the 'Jim Crow' laws that began after the American Civil War, and continued into the 1960s.

On many American college campuses, students from all backgrounds began to hold demonstrations against apartheid to draw public attention to the injustices that people suffered under these laws. The political group in which Barry was involved had invited a representative from the African National Congress (ANC) to speak at Occidental College. The group had concocted a plan to dramatize the plight of native South Africans. The students decided that before the representative spoke, Barry should make some opening remarks. Then a group of white students dressed in military garb would rush up to the stage and drag him away to highlight how black people in South Africa were denied their right to speak.

Remembering his father's talk to Miss Hefty's class, it suddenly dawned on Barry what he wanted to say.

He began by pointing out that the struggle in South Africa was one that was truly relevant to each student on the campus. It may have been happening on another continent, but it was the kind of issue that meant that everyone needed to know where they stood. Did they support dignity, fairness and commitment? Or did they believe in injustice?

Barry's words demanded the attention of everyone. And as he continued speaking, it became so quiet you could have heard a pin drop. He was challenging everyone there to be aware that this was *their* struggle too – that it was time to choose sides.

But as planned, his friends ran onto the stage and began dragging him away. Barry struggled to stay. It was what they had agreed to do, but he did not want to leave the stage. He had a captive audience. He had seen the reaction of the crowd to his short speech. They were cheering and urging him on. They wanted to hear more. He desperately wanted to continue speaking, but his friends were following the script.

Barry reluctantly allowed himself to be dragged off the stage. The guest speakers took over and began delivering their speeches. Some of the students who had stopped when he spoke went back to playing frisbee, and the enthusiasm that Barry had generated with his inspiring words was lost.

He realized that he had a gift – the rich, musical voice that he had inherited from his father. He recalled his father's visit to Miss Hefty's class, when everyone had listened, spellbound.

Another revelation soon followed. Barry understood that it was time for him to start using the name given to him at birth: a name that identified who he was – *Barack*, a blessing in his father's native Swahili tongue.

CHAPTER NINE

'Meaningful change always begins at the grassroots . . .'

After spending two years at Occidental College, Barack transferred to Columbia University in New York City. He felt that he was not getting enough out of his education. He wanted to study politics and to live among people whose lives he wanted to understand and help improve. He chose Columbia University because it was located near Harlem, a neighbourhood famous for its black culture and crowded slums. He wanted to live somewhere where he would be in touch with people like himself.

Under the clear night sky, curled up in a Harlem alleyway, was where Barack spent his first night in New York City. He had made arrangements to stay with a friend, but when he arrived and knocked on the door, no one answered. Barack did not have enough money to stay at a local hotel. So he made a pillow with his luggage and settled in with the sounds of the city all around him. In the morning when he woke up, he joined a homeless man at the street fire hydrant, where they both washed themselves.

Barack quickly settled into Columbia University and the big city life. He put all his energy into his studies. When he was not in class or in his flat studying, he walked the streets, looking at the way in which the poor people lived.

He became more and more disturbed by what he saw. Tenement buildings in desperate need of repair. Drunks on street corners, bleary-eyed and sad. Drug dealers in pursuit of yet another client. He wondered if he could find a way to help turn their lives around. He saw none.

Barack had found a job working on a

construction site in order to pay his bills and buy enough food to get by. He found it amazing that many black people were living in poverty and degradation in a rich country like the USA. America was supposed to be founded on the principle that all people were created equal. Why then were so many people living outside the American dream of equality and freedom? He asked himself many questions for which he did not yet have answers.

Barack told his mother that he was planning to visit Africa to see his father the following year. Ann was very pleased that her son was still in contact with his dad. She had always worked hard to encourage communication between father and son. But during the planning stages of his trip, Barack received a shocking phone call from Kenya from his Aunt Jane, with the terrible news that his father had died in a car accident. His father was 46 years old.

Barack had lost his father at the age of 21. He did not attend the funeral in Africa, but he sent his condolences to the family.

Faced with this devastating loss, he directed his pent-up pain and disappointment along a specific path. He decided on a career in public service like his father, but in the area of community action. Here, he could work directly with people to help organize themselves into improving their life chances. He saw that this strategy, if done effectively, could bring poor people – regardless of the colour of their skin – together to work for their common good. It could bridge the financial and social gaps between those who were privileged and those who were not.

When his college classmates questioned his choice of career, he told them that America needed change – change not just in the laws of the government, but change in the way that Americans thought about themselves. He argued that such change could not come from the top, which had a vested interest in the status quo. It had to come from the bottom. The grassroots. These were the people he would organize. His friends politely listened to his plans and then went about their business.

As his last year at Columbia came to a close, Barack wrote letters to countless community organizations and progressive politicians, seeking employment with them. The responses were all negative. Because he needed to earn a living, he took a job as a research assistant with a company that published financial reports. The job paid very well and he finally had enough money to live comfortably. He was the only black person in the company who was not a janitor or a secretary. When he told some of his co-workers that he intended to become a community organizer, they thought he was mad. They wondered why he would leave such a well-paid job to work with the powerless in the poor neighbourhoods. 'You're going to be sorry one day,' one of them warned.

Another co-worker advised him, 'Forget about this organizing business and do something that's going to make you some money'. Barack's plan was not about how much *money* he could make but how much of a *difference* he could make.

Finally, a civil rights organization offered Barack a job. It would involve attending conferences that dealt with drugs, unemployment and unfair housing laws in New York City. Barack turned the job down, as impressive as it was, because he did not want to work in boardrooms discussing problems. He wanted to be directly involved in solving the problems.

Broke and unemployed, he waited. Then one day he got a call from a man who had started a church-based community organization in Chicago, Illinois. He was looking for a trainee. He offered Barack a very small salary of $10,000 a year, and an allowance of $2,000 to buy a car.

Barack grasped the opportunity. He packed up his few belongings, tossed them into the old used car he bought, and headed west.

CHAPTER TEN

'I'll never forget that my journey began on the streets of Chicago . . . organizing, and working, and fighting to make people's lives just a little bit better.'

Barack Obama had visited Chicago only once, with his mother and grandmother when he was eleven years old. On his return, he was coming not as a visitor but as an agent of change. He wondered where he would start.

Two years before Barack arrived, Chicago had elected its first African American mayor, who worked hard to improve the lives of those in the city. But there was a great deal of poverty there because many people, white and black, had lost their jobs when two large employers – US Steel and Wisconsin Steel – closed. Around the same time, many other factories also shut down.

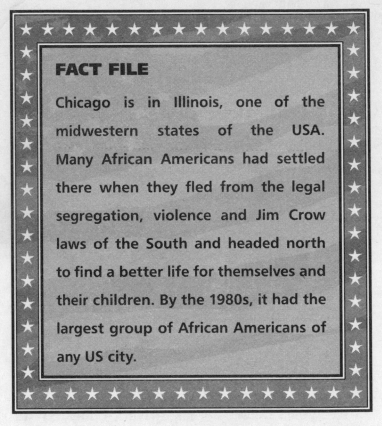

FACT FILE

Chicago is in Illinois, one of the midwestern states of the USA. Many African Americans had settled there when they fled from the legal segregation, violence and Jim Crow laws of the South and headed north to find a better life for themselves and their children. By the 1980s, it had the largest group of African Americans of any US city.

Barack's first job was working with residents at a public housing project. The buildings sat between the polluted Calumet River on one side and the Lake Calumet landfill, an enormous dump, on the other. The stench from the city's sewage plant hung constantly in the air. In his little office in a local church, Barack set to work. He listened and he learned. He learned that what people wanted most of all was to get jobs. Unemployment was high and there was no opportunity for training in the neighbourhood. Many young men, with nothing to do, joined gangs and fell into trouble.

With a group of dedicated helpers, Barack began his work.

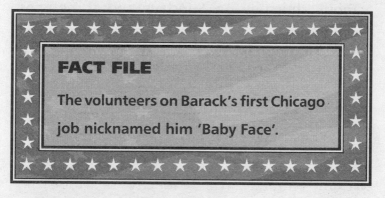

FACT FILE

The volunteers on Barack's first Chicago job nicknamed him 'Baby Face'.

He was young, intense and lacking in experience. He tried working with the churches in an effort to get them to join forces and become organized in the community, but they had their own ways of working. Eventually, after many months of hard work, the Chicago city government agreed to open a Community Office of Employment and Training. Progress had begun, but there was much more to be done.

Barack had never felt a need for religion in his life. He had not grown up in any religious tradition. However, he noticed that many of his volunteers were churchgoers who seemed to gain some strength from their church and the church communities. He began to drop in to various churches on Sundays and sometimes talked to the pastors. He grew attached to the Trinity United Church. The pastor, Jeremiah Wright, a very intelligent and charismatic preacher, was committed to social justice. There was a sign on the lawn protesting against apartheid in South Africa. One sermon by Wright entitled 'The Audacity of Hope', in which he spoke about injustice, violence and suffering in the world and also in their own neighbourhood, moved Barack to tears.

During his time as a community organizer, Barack's half-sister Auma – the daughter of his father's first wife in Kenya – visited him in

Chicago. She was living in Germany. They felt close to each other as soon as they met. Auma unfolded many stories of his family in Africa. She told him about his father, his other siblings and the reality of family life in Kenya. Although Barack Sr had got into high office on his return to Kenya, he had lost favour when tribal differences caused conflict in the country. Barack and his sister agreed to travel to Kenya and to visit the family together.

Barack continued his work and learned many lessons working as a community organizer.

He stated that: 'If there is a child on the South Side of Chicago who can't read, that matters to me . . . If there is a senior citizen somewhere who can't pay for her prescription and has to choose between medicine and the rent, that makes my life poorer . . . If there is an Arab American family being rounded up without benefit of an attorney or due process, that threatens my civil liberties.'

Twenty years later, when he announced to the nation that he was running for the presidency, he used these years as a community organizer to press home his point. 'I learned that meaningful change always begins at the grassroots, and that engaged citizens working together can accomplish extraordinary things.'

Eventually, his hard work began to pay off. Groups began to form and work together. Streets were being repaired, toilets fixed and rubbish collected. Politicians began to hear his name and tried to find out who he was. He received invitations to speak on panels to discuss what was wrong in the communities.

Barack had become a leader. People came to him to discuss solutions to their problems. They asked for advice on political issues. People began to speak of him even if they still had trouble with his name.

It was his work as a community organizer that helped Barack realize that if he went into politics he might be able to help more people and effect more changes in society.

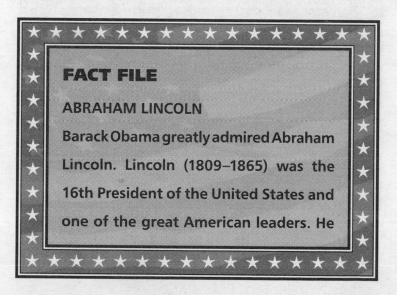

FACT FILE

ABRAHAM LINCOLN

Barack Obama greatly admired Abraham Lincoln. Lincoln (1809–1865) was the 16th President of the United States and one of the great American leaders. He introduced measures that resulted in the abolition of slavery. When he was elected President, seven southern states left the Union and the American Civil War followed. The fighting began in 1861 and went on for four long years. In January 1863, Lincoln issued the Emancipation Proclamation, which freed all slaves, and the war became a struggle to end slavery. Lincoln was assassinated in 1865, just after the war had been won.

Barack Obama used Lincoln's Bible to swear his Oath of Allegiance when he won the Presidency himself.

CHAPTER ELEVEN

'I feel comfortable in my own skin.'

Barack was 26 years old when he boarded a plane to travel to Kenya. He wanted to visit his father's country before he progressed with his career.

When he landed at the airport and searched for his Aunt Zeituni and sister Auma, he felt the same anxiety he had experienced many years before when he had paused outside of his grandparents' apartment feeling reluctant to go inside and meet his father. Would he get on with these new-found relatives? Would they even like him? What if he had made a mistake in coming to Kenya?

His fears came to an abrupt end when Aunt Zeituni and Auma welcomed him with warm embraces and said in unison, 'Welcome home!' in Swahili. Aunt Zeituni told Auma, 'Do not let him get lost again.'

Barack did not think that he was lost, but Auma explained that 'getting lost' meant that they did not want to lose him now that they had met him and that they wanted to always be in touch with him in the future.

Barack felt at home in Kenya. He looked like everyone else on the streets. His hair was curly like theirs and so were his eyelashes. If only his friends in Jakarta could be here, they would have many people to call 'Curly Eyelashes'.

When Barack awoke on his first morning and went outdoors, he saw a troop of monkeys looking at him. They roamed free. They were not like the ones in Indonesia that were owned by humans, nor were they like Tata. He wondered what had become of his pet.

Barack met countless relatives. A grandmother, uncles, aunts, brothers, nieces and nephews, and cousins galore. He met Aunt Jane, who had called to tell him of his father's death. They sat down for a meal that Barack would remember like the ones in Indonesia and Hawaii. They ate curried goat, collard greens, fried fish and ugali, made from corn.

In Kenya, family is very important and there are responsibilities for certain members. The successful ones are expected to help the less fortunate. It was also expected that the ones who had travelled abroad should visit every family member when they returned. So Barack hit the road with Auma. They covered many miles. Everyone he met treated him with love and respect. They asked many questions about his life in the cold place called Chicago and what it was like being a community organizer.

Although Kenya was a fascinating and lovely place, Barack saw similarities with the neighbourhoods in Chicago. There was poverty and hopelessness here too. There were people in the Chicago slums who suffered in the cold. Those in Kenya's slums suffered in the heat.

Most importantly, Barack learned more about his father.

He met many people who knew and had respected Barack Sr. And he found out that his father had experienced a great deal of success when he returned from America in 1965, holding down a good job with an American petroleum company based in Kenya. This had been followed by appointments in the Kenyan government. He lived in a large house and drove an expensive car. From the letters his father had written to him, however, Barack had never heard about the hard times that followed.

Auma explained to him part of the reason why his father had fallen out of favour and ended up poor. She said that the then head of state, Jomo Kenyatta, favoured the Kikuyu tribe and promoted them into positions of power over the Luo, Barack's father's tribe. His father had complained, and he had then been sacked from his position in the Kenyan Ministry of Finance. Afterwards, he hadn't been able to find work. He grew bitter and quarrelsome. The wife he had married after his divorce from Ann left him. His children had helped as much as they could, but his situation became very bad. He had a series of car accidents, and finally died in one.

One of the highlights of Barack's visit to Kenya was a safari with Auma. He was delighted when he saw up close the same animals his father had talked about in Miss Hefty's class back in Hawaii when he was a boy. He saw gazelles, wildebeest, giraffes, zebras and once in a while a Masai herdsman in the company of a herd of cattle.

In his grandmother's house in a village called Kogelo, Barack gained insights into the lives of his relations. At every turn, there were family photographs and even a copy of his father's doctorate degree from Harvard University hanging on a wall. His grandmother gave him the long version of his family's history. He learned so much in that short time.

Barack forgave his father for being absent in his life. He knelt at his grave and the tears came. He realized that his father had been human and subject to mistakes and bad judgements, just like anyone else. His father, he concluded, had not been just a distant memory, but a real person.

CHAPTER TWELVE

'For every one of me, there are hundreds or thousands of black students with at least equal talents who don't get a chance . . .'

Even before he visited Kenya, Barack had become frustrated with the situation in Chicago. Poor people on the South Side were still suffering, and those in power – 'the conventional politicians', he called them – were good at saying that 'this law' or 'that rule' prevented them from making important reforms.

He realized that, if he really wanted to bring about any change in society, he had to totally understand how to use the law to get things done. It was time to go back to school – to get a law degree.

Barack was accepted at several law schools, but he decided to go to the same institution that his father had attended: Harvard University in Boston. At the age of 27, he was among the older students in his class. He was also well disciplined and committed to serious study.

Harvard is a very privileged place, with beautiful buildings and well-tended grounds. After living in Chicago and New York, this environment made Barack feel uncomfortable. He chose to rent a basement apartment in a racially mixed, working-class community nearby. While committed to studying and making his mark academically at the university, he devoted considerable time to student activity.

Black students at Harvard were asking for more representation on campus, and Barack gave a speech about the issue. From his training as a community organizer, he knew the importance of finding common ground, so that people could think through an issue, rather than shout slogans at each other.

His involvement in debates made a considerable difference. He was able to get his fellow students to drop all the emotion and focus on the facts, using well chosen, balanced arguments. Remembering his impact on fellow students, one member of his class recalled how Barack had seemed mature beyond his years in the way he approached issues. And one administrator at Harvard even foretold the future by recognizing that Barack was the kind of guy who he would like to see as a President.

Barack made national news for the first time when he became the president of the *Harvard Law Review* magazine. In an interview following his election, he told a newspaper reporter, 'The fact that I've been elected shows a great deal of progress. It's encouraging. But it's important that stories like mine aren't used to say that everything is OK for blacks. You have to remember that for every one of me, there are hundreds or thousands of black students with at least equal talents who don't get a chance.'

Working closely with Harvard professors on

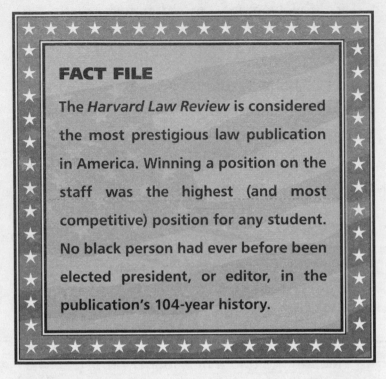

FACT FILE

The *Harvard Law Review* is considered the most prestigious law publication in America. Winning a position on the staff was the highest (and most competitive) position for any student. No black person had ever before been elected president, or editor, in the publication's 104-year history.

the *Law Review*, he won their respect for his common sense as well as his knowledge. 'He was the kind of person who you knew was destined for greatness,' one professor commented.

Barack had become not only a powerful speaker, but also an engaging writer. He made even the boring and abstract topics published in the *Law Review* sound interesting.

He spent three years at law school. By the time he graduated from Harvard in 1991, at the age of 30, Barack had made a name for himself and there were job offers from high-level law firms around the country.

He turned them all down and returned, as promised, to Chicago and the mission for which he was training himself. A career in politics.

Over the following year, he directed a state-wide voter registration drive called 'Project Vote'. 150,000 people who had never voted before were now registered to vote in elections.

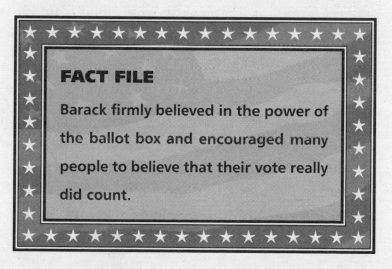

FACT FILE

Barack firmly believed in the power of the ballot box and encouraged many people to believe that their vote really did count.

Changes were now taking place in other parts of America. Among the winners in the 1993 elections was Carol Moseley Braun, Illinois' first African-American senator and the first black woman ever elected to the US Senate in Washington, DC. She held the post until 1999.

Following the elections, Barack joined a civil rights law firm in Chicago and worked on discrimination cases to help the poor. One of his professors at Harvard told a colleague at the University of Chicago that a 'really brilliant' young lawyer was living in Chicago and should be teaching at the university. This led to Barack's appointment as lecturer at the University of Chicago, where he taught law between 1993 and 2004.

The appointment came complete with a small room near the law library. Here, Barack began writing. He intended to write about race relations in America but came up with something much more personal – a memoir of his life and family. He called it *Dreams From My Father: A Story of Race and Inheritance*.

CHAPTER THIRTEEN

'The rock of our family, the love of my life, the nation's next First Lady: Michelle Obama.'

In the summer of 1989, Michelle Robinson had just finished her first year as an associate at Sidley & Austin, a law firm in Chicago, when the firm assigned her to mentor a summer associate named Barack Obama. Summer associate programmes are a form of work experience that gives students a hands-on introduction to the work of a company. Even before he arrived, there was much talk at the firm about this brilliant young man from Harvard Law School.

Michelle, who had recently graduated from Harvard herself, was annoyed by all the gossip. Why were people so surprised that a black man could be smart and capable?

Michelle was less interested in his competence than by his odd name and in the fact that he had grown up in Hawaii. Her guess was that he would be 'a little nerdy, a little strange', and that she was not sure that she would like him.

Michelle was born in Chicago on 17 January 1964. She grew up in a working-class black neighbourhood called South Shore. Her father, Fraser Robinson, was a city water employee whose great-grandfather had been a slave in the state of South Carolina. Michelle was enrolled in gifted classes in elementary school and graduated with honours from Whitney Young High School. She attended Princeton University, an old and elite university near New York City, before being accepted to Harvard Law School. She graduated in 1988, the same year that Barack had travelled to Kenya to visit his late father's relatives.

Her reservations about Barack immediately

disappeared when she met him. Barack, too, was very impressed with Michelle from the first time he saw her. But they both felt a bit hesitant about getting involved with each other. Michelle thought it might be 'tacky' if they started dating because they were among the very few black professionals at the firm.

At last Barack won Michelle over, and they went on their first date to an ice cream shop. They both had their favourite flavour. Chocolate. Not long after, Barack took her to a meeting with a group of people he had worked with as a community organizer before he started law school. When Michelle got into his car, she couldn't help but notice that there was a large rust hole in the passenger door. The car shook violently as it started up, and she thought, 'This brother is not interested in ever making a dime.'

At the meeting Barack stood up and spoke words that swept Michelle off her feet. 'He talked about the world as it is, and the world as it should be. And he said that, all too often, we accept the distance between the two, and we settle for the world as it is, even when it doesn't reflect our values and aspirations. I knew then and there that Barack Obama was the real deal.'

She took him to meet her family. Her older brother, Craig, had been a star basketball player at Princeton University, and he took Barack to the ball court to test his skill and his character. Barack passed with flying colours. Craig reported back to his sister that he was self-confident but not a 'ball hog' or 'hotshot'. Barack went back to Harvard, and the couple began a long-distance relationship until he graduated.

On 18 October 1992, they married at Trinity United Church of Christ in Chicago. Many family members attended the ceremony, including Barack's mother, Ann, and his sisters, Auma and Maya. After a honeymoon in California, the couple moved into an apartment building in Hyde Park, a South Side neighbourhood near the University of Chicago.

The couple were eager to pursue their goals as agents of change. Michelle resigned from her job and started working for the city of

Chicago. Soon she was promoted to what she considered a 'dream' job as city economic development coordinator, which connected her to efforts to bring jobs to poorer neighbourhoods.

FACT FILE

A political campaign means the candidate has to go out to meet voters and to persuade them that he or she is the right person to represent them. It involves making speeches at different events, running TV ads and doing whatever is necessary to get their message across to the people. In the USA, campaigning can be very expensive and volunteer help is often involved. A presidential campaign can cost as much as 200 million dollars!

Barack, meanwhile, had decided to run for public office. This meant being chosen as a member of the local government, which makes decisions on state laws. He began to campaign.

But there was a very sad and difficult time for him first. On 7 November 1995, his mother died. She was 52 years old. Ann had fought a long battle with cancer.

Barack returned to Hawaii and, accompanied by Maya, spread Ann's ashes over the Pacific Ocean on the south side of Oahu. The loss of his mother affected him deeply, as Barack knew how much he owed to her – and to her kindness and generosity.

In that same year his autobiography, *Dreams From My Father*, was published. In 1996, he joined the legislature as the representative for the same South Side district where he had worked as a community organizer and where he now lived with Michelle. In his first two terms in the Illinois government – a period of nearly five years – he was able to get many laws passed. He achieved this, even though his party, the

Democratic Party, was outnumbered by the Opposition – the Republican Party.

FACT FILE

In the USA, the two major political parties are the Republicans and the Democrats. They are broadly similar in approach to the Conservatives and Labour in the UK. Ex-President Bush was a Republican. Barack Obama is a Democrat.

Part of his success as a legislator was his ability to reach across the political divide and forge friendships with his opponents. This was the same tactic he had used as a community organizer and as president of the *Harvard Law Review*. Barack got along well with people from all parts of Chicago society. Although the city had a history of racial intolerance, he felt that he understood the white voters. They reminded him of Gramps and Toot.

Obama impressed many legislators with his hard work and commitment to getting things done. One Republican state senator commented on how many senators had originally resented Obama – his intelligence and articulate debating skills – but he noted how this new arrival in Springfield (the Illinois state capital) also turned up at all the meetings he needed to. Obama gave the impression of a man destined for success. And one prepared to work for it.

In 1999, Michelle gave birth to their first child. They named her Malia Ann.

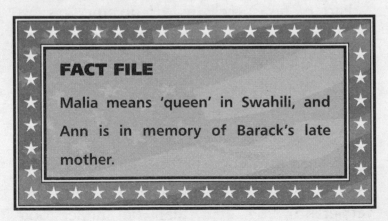

FACT FILE

Malia means 'queen' in Swahili, and Ann is in memory of Barack's late mother.

Barack was delighted to be a father and determined to do his best for his child.

In 2000, he decided to run for a seat in the US House of Representatives. This position would allow him to be the voice of the South Side in Washington DC, where Congress makes laws for the entire nation.

His opponent was a powerful black politician named Bobby Rush, who had held the House seat since 1993 and was running for his fifth term. Trying to defeat someone already in power, especially a popular incumbent, was very difficult. Rush had been a member of the Black Panther political group in the 1960s and was respected and experienced in Chicago politics.

Barack thought that Rush did a poor job of representing the district and tried to discuss the issues. Rush hit back by accusing him of being an elitist who was 'not black enough' because he had attended fancy universities. Obama responded by citing his history of organizing poor residents, but Rush's line of attack was very effective.

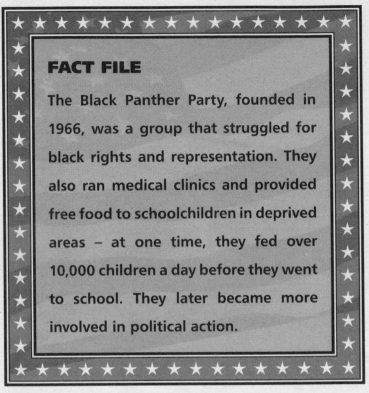

FACT FILE

The Black Panther Party, founded in 1966, was a group that struggled for black rights and representation. They also ran medical clinics and provided free food to schoolchildren in deprived areas – at one time, they fed over 10,000 children a day before they went to school. They later became more involved in political action.

Rush beat Obama by a two-to-one margin. Barack was devastated and wondered if he should even continue with his dream.

It was 2001 and the Obamas welcomed a second daughter into the world. They named her Natasha. She was nicknamed Sasha. Barack now had to carve out more time from his busy schedule to devote to his family – a family that meant the world to him.

CHAPTER FOURTEEN

'There are some people who won't vote for me because I'm black. There would also be some people who won't vote for me because I'm young, because I've got big ears ... or because they don't like my political philosophy.'

Barack did not just lose the race to Bobby Rush. He had, he felt, been rejected by voters. His defeat led one political commentator in Chicago to wonder out loud: 'Is Obama dead?'

This was a low point in his life. He and Michelle were in debt because Barack had used some of their personal money to finance his campaign.

When he tried to rent a car to attend a political event, his credit card was rejected. At this point he could have decided that the rough-and-tumble world of politics was not for him. After all, he had a prestigious job at the University of Chicago and could always work for a big salary as a private lawyer. In other words, he could have given up, or sulked, or blamed voters for not recognizing his political talents.

But he did nothing of the kind.

He would not be thrown out of a game for which he had carefully prepared himself. Instead, he pulled himself together and undertook the work of state senator in Springfield with renewed energy.

A year after his defeat by Bobby Rush, another fateful event occurred that would call into question his ambitions for higher office. On 11 September 2001, followers of terrorist Osama bin Laden attacked the World Trade Center in New York City. Thousands of people were killed. Many ordinary Americans became suspicious of anyone with a name that suggested a link to the Muslim or Arab world. 'The conventional wisdom was that no one named Barack Hussein Obama was going to be elected to Congress after 9/11,' said David Axelrod, a political consultant in Chicago.

When the US President, George W. Bush, ordered the military invasion of Iraq in 2002, Barack was one of the first elected American politicians to question the decision. He said clearly that he was not a pacifist, or a person who considered all wars to be wrong. He believed, for example, that the American Civil War, which freed black slaves, was morally justified. 'I am not opposed to all wars. I'm opposed to dumb wars,' he said. Invading Iraq was dumb, he explained, because it did not combat the true threat facing America – namely, terrorist groups such as Al-Qaeda run by Osama bin Laden – and because he feared that the invasion would cause a civil war among factions in Iraq.

But it was not just foreign policy that worried Barack. He found himself increasingly at odds with the current administration on economic and social issues. He believed, for example, that the national government was ignoring the problems of working families and allowing big corporations to take jobs out of America. And he was horrified by a $1.35 trillion tax-cut bill, which President Bush signed in 2001, that gave the bulk of the tax cuts to already wealthy households.

Barack Obama began looking for another way in which he could make a difference in society.

One way was to try again for national office. In 2004, a US Senate seat for Illinois was up for grabs and he believed he had a chance of winning the position, which would make him one of two senators who represented Illinois in Washington.

But first he had to win the support of Michelle, who was concerned about raising two young girls while her husband was out campaigning. She listened to his reasoning and reluctantly agreed to his plan, but not before warning him, jokingly, that he shouldn't necessarily count on her vote!

Learning from his campaign against Bobby Rush, Barack laid out a careful plan to be chosen by his party – the Democrats – to be their candidate for the seat. He hired David Axelrod, an experienced political consultant, to run his campaign staff. Although voters in the city of Chicago recognized his name, he also needed to win the support of predominately white and rural voters in 'downstate' Illinois if he was to be victorious.

This time he was confident that he could speak to average Americans. His deadpan sense of humour, long known to friends, became a good way to 'break the ice' when he travelled to farming districts far from Chicago.

He typically began his speech by saying that people were always getting his name wrong, calling him 'Yo Mama' or 'Alabama'. The crowds roared with laughter. Then he took on the question of racial difference head on, declaring, 'We have shared values, values that aren't black or white or Hispanic – values that are American.'

Obama led a 'grassroots' campaign. Relying on volunteers and word-of-mouth publicity, he made steady headway over many months of campaigning. Voters began to talk about 'the skinny guy with the funny name', who seemed to really mean what he said about reform.

In March 2004, he stunned the political world by beating six other Democratic Party candidates and receiving 53% of the vote. His victory was covered by a Honolulu newspaper which said it all: 'PUNAHOU GRAD STIRS UP ILLINOIS POLITICS.'

Politics in America is a hard grind, and after winning the selection as the Democratic Party candidate, Obama still had to face the Republican Party candidate in the general election in November 2003.

The Republicans, the opposing party, picked a wealthy businessman named Jack Ryan. He suggested that Obama was as dangerous to US security as the terrorist leader Osama bin Laden. Ryan hired a cameraman who followed Barack around and taped everything he said, standing as close as possible to his face. Obama's legendary self-control was sorely tested by these encounters, but he kept his cool.

Ryan had to withdraw from the race after his campaign tumbled into trouble. Desperate to find another candidate, the Republican Party recruited Alan Keyes, a black politician known for his extreme conservative opinions. Keyes ranted against Obama and made bizarre comments that turned off voters, saying, for example, that Jesus Christ wouldn't vote for Obama. The Keyes tactics backfired.

The skinny guy with the funny name won by a landslide, achieving a majority of votes from every region of Illinois.

In January 2005, Obama became the fifth African American to occupy a seat in the US Senate, the upper chamber of Congress.

A few days before his swearing-in ceremony, he and Michelle arrived in Washington. As they took the lift to their hotel room, Michelle recalled the events leading up to winning the primary and then the general election. 'We got off the elevator,' Barack told an interviewer, 'and she looked me at me and said, "I can't believe you pulled it off."'

CHAPTER FIFTEEN

'To be the only African American in [the US Senate] is a tremendous responsibility.'

In the middle of his campaign, Barack Obama returned to Boston and, just a few miles from where he had attended law school at Harvard, he delivered a speech that would for ever change his life. The date was 24 July 2004, and the speech was at the Democratic National Convention.

Every four years, the two major political parties in the USA – the Democrats and the Republicans – hold meetings to nominate their candidates for President and Vice President of the United States. Senator John Kerry of Massachusetts, the Democratic presidential nominee, had heard good things about Obama and asked him to give the keynote address. Some members of Kerry's staff were worried about giving 'prime-time' exposure to a man largely unknown outside the state of Illinois. One of them fretted that Obama might fluff the speech.

They had no need to panic.

In the first few sentences, Obama laid down the groundwork for his ideas for a better America. He talked about his black father who 'got a scholarship to study in a magical place, America, that shone as a beacon of freedom and opportunity', and about his white grandfather, Gramps, who worked on oil rigs as a teenager and served in the military in the Second World War.

Instead of directly criticizing the current President, George W. Bush, Obama spoke of the core values that united Americans. These small miracles, he declared, included the expectation that 'we can tuck in our children at night and know that they are fed and clothed and safe from harm' and that 'we can say what we think, write what we think, without hearing a sudden knock on the door' – a subtle but powerful rebuke of the erosion of American liberties under the Bush administration since 9/11.

Just like the students who had stopped playing frisbee to hear Barack speak about apartheid at Occidental College, the 5,000 delegates in Boston took notice as he urged Americans to come together to tackle common problems. Many political commentators, he pointed out, 'like to slice and dice our country into Red [Republican] States and Blue [Democratic] States'. But Obama had news for them: 'There's not a liberal America and a conservative America – there's the United States of America.'

The speech was hailed as one of the best and most inspirational speeches in recent American history. Contributions to Obama's campaign started flowing in and he acquired 14 million dollars to move forward with his plans. Despite the colour of his skin and his unusual name, people were excited by his message of hope.

John Kerry lost to George Bush in the 2004 presidential election, but Obama emerged as a rising star in the Democratic Party. As he jokingly told another journalist, using basketball slang, 'I got game!'

Rising star or not, when he was at home in Chicago, Barack had to wash the dishes after dinner, take the children to school and ride with them in bumper cars at the fair.

He followed a hectic schedule as a new US senator. He lived alone in a rented flat in Washington and commuted back to Chicago for long weekends and Congressional holidays. Michelle took over childcare duties, relying on her family for support.

Even from afar, Michelle kept her husband grounded to the daily challenges of running a household. When he telephoned her from Washington to share the good news that a law he had worked on had been approved, she interrupted him with: 'We have ants. I found ants in the kitchen. And in the bathroom upstairs. I need you to buy some ant traps on your way home tomorrow.'

Recounting this episode, Obama said that he hung up the receiver wondering if Ted Kennedy or John McCain [two other US senators] had to buy ant traps on their way home from work!

While in Washington, he seldom attended the fancy social balls for which the capital city is famous. Instead, he typically read through bills and worked late into the night. To relax, he played basketball at the Senate gym or jogged the two miles from the Capitol building to the Lincoln Memorial.

Obama used his experience as a community organizer and his time working at the *Harvard Law Review* to approach and engage members of the Republican Party in his vision for the future. He believed that the only way to get things done was to involve the other party.

He visited the Lincoln Memorial, the place where Abraham Lincoln – the great President who in 1865 introduced the Thirteenth Amendment to the US Constitution, abolishing slavery in the USA – is buried, and stood on the spot where in 1963 Martin Luther King Jr delivered his 'I Have a Dream' speech. These places were important to Barack Obama. He felt a special connection with both Lincoln and King, pioneers in the cause of American racial justice, who both became martyrs, killed by assassins who hated the very notion that 'all men were created equal'.

Barack recounted feelings like these in his book *The Audacity of Hope*, published in the autumn of 2006. The book immediately became a number one bestseller.

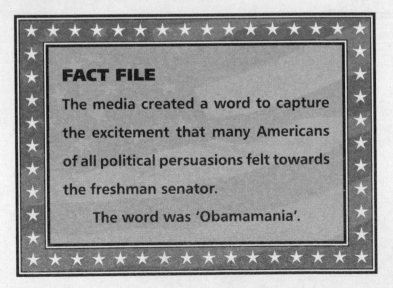

FACT FILE

The media created a word to capture the excitement that many Americans of all political persuasions felt towards the freshman senator.

The word was 'Obamamania'.

CHAPTER SIXTEEN

'The decision to run for President is a very serious one. And it's a very humbling decision. I have to feel that I have something unique to offer the country that no other person can provide.'

Michelle: *You need to ask yourself, why do you want to do this? What are you hoping to uniquely accomplish, Barack?*

Barack: *This I know: when I raise my hand and take that Oath of Office, I think the world will look at us differently. And millions of kids across the country will look at themselves differently.*

Barack and Michelle had this conversation many times before finally, on 10 February 2007, an icy cold winter's day, they took the plunge. With Michelle at his side, Barack Obama announced his candidacy for the highest elected office in America. His speech was said to be the most prolific, honest and historic in American political history. The setting, in Springfield, Illinois, was significant because it was there that Abraham Lincoln had delivered his famous warning that 'a house divided against itself cannot stand'.

The issue shaking the nation when Lincoln spoke was the practice of slavery. Now a new set of issues threatened to weaken and divide America, and Barack told an enthusiastic crowd, 'All of us know what those challenges are today – a war with no end, a dependence on oil that threatens our future, schools where too many children aren't learning, and families struggling from paycheck to paycheck despite working as hard as they can.'

When asked about Obama's readiness for the candidacy, a reporter quipped: 'I don't want to wait until he is ready. I'm ready for Barack Obama. Because things are going to hell in a hand basket.'

After describing the nation's problems, Obama asked the crowd if, together, they could bring about change and achieve Lincoln's 'more perfect union'. He pointed out that 'there has never been anything false about hope'. He reminded them that 'when we have faced impossible odds, when we've been told that we're not ready, or that we shouldn't try, or that we can't, generations of Americans have responded with a simple creed that sums up the spirit of a people. Yes we can.'

David Axelrod, Obama's chief strategist, had devised that slogan, 'Yes we can', for the presidential campaign. At first, Barack didn't like the slogan. He thought that it was not powerful enough, but he realized that it registered strongly with the crowds when he began campaigning in Iowa, the state where the first votes for the Democratic Party nomination would be cast.

Under the American election system, a

presidential candidate has to win the nomination of his or her party before running in the general election. For Obama that meant elections in all 50 states against other Democratic contenders.

He faced a very competent group of rivals. Among the top two Democrats running for President were John Edwards, who was the vice-presidential running mate of John Kerry in 2004, and Hillary Rodham Clinton, who had spent eight years in the White House while her husband, Bill Clinton, was President. Mrs Clinton was herself on a historic quest to become the first female President of the United States.

In the early days of the campaign, polls showed that two out of three American voters had little or no idea who Barack Obama was. That changed as Obama mobilized his supporters, using a visitor-friendly website and related networking sites developed by Facebook and YouTube.

Mrs Clinton accused him of having too few legislative accomplishments to run for President and of being too naïve. But Obama argued that he had detailed proposals for solving major problems, such as poor health care. To the criticism by Mrs Clinton and others that he was not 'tough enough' to be President, Obama responded with humour:

'Listen, I'm a black guy named Barack Obama running for President. You want to tell me that I'm not tough enough?'

A campaign needs money, and Barack started receiving small contributions from people who had never before been active in politics.

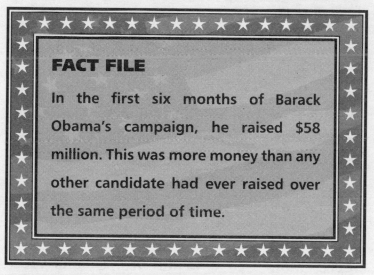

FACT FILE

In the first six months of Barack Obama's campaign, he raised $58 million. This was more money than any other candidate had ever raised over the same period of time.

As the race went on, John Edwards dropped out, and Obama was left to run against Hillary Clinton. While Clinton relied on traditional party members to get out and vote, Obama leaned on the enthusiasm and computer savvy of his volunteers. Slowly, Obama moved into the lead.

Many people who had just assumed that a black man could not win national office were taking a new look. Obama showed strength among white voters, especially among the young and better-educated. For example, he won in Iowa, where only 2.5% of the population is African American.

Obama ran an upbeat, disciplined campaign that led to his nickname among reporters as 'No-Drama Obama'. He did not allow anything negative to stop him, including false rumours that he was somehow associated with 'anti-American' groups.

During a rally in Minnesota, one woman took the microphone and announced, 'I can't trust Obama. He's an Arab.' Unaffected by mis-representation of who he was, Obama went from state to state, from neighbourhood to neighbourhood, sometimes from door to door, delivering his message of hope and change.

Wherever he went, people showed up – first in hundreds, then in thousands and then in tens of thousands. Not just African Americans, but white and brown people, old and young, and Americans from all different social backgrounds and religious beliefs came to hear him speak.

Obama fought a good fight and won another improbable victory. He was the Democratic Party's nominee for President. He defeated Hillary Clinton and she now threw her support behind him. Many observers thought he would pick her as his vice-presidential running mate, but instead he chose Joseph Biden, a US senator from Delaware. Biden brought with him years of experience in foreign affairs and was also opposed to the war in Iraq.

As their candidate for the presidency, the Republican Party nominated John W. McCain, a US Senator from Arizona and one of the most vocal defenders of the Iraq War. McCain denounced Obama as 'a free-spending liberal' who wanted government to interfere in the lives of ordinary citizens. That kind of approach had worked well for Republicans for many years, but Obama was prepared with a response. He argued that what he really wanted was for government to serve the needs of the Americans who were being squeezed by job losses and a sick economy. Obama's point was dramatized when a major US financial company collapsed just days before the candidates held a debate on national television.

Obama's calm and confident presentation during the debate won him new supporters. He never mocked his opponent to gain favour with the voters. In fact, he made it a point to inform voters where he agreed with McCain. However, whenever necessary he would stand his ground if he felt that he was being unfairly treated.

'I believe that we are not as divided as our politics suggests; that the dreams we share are more powerful than the differences we have – because I am living proof of that ideal,' he said.

On the campaign trail many candidates fail to eat properly. They succumb to the junk food that is readily available, like chips, burgers and waffles. But Barack would push these foods away and eat the same meal almost every day – grilled salmon and broccoli. He kept fit by playing pick-up basketball with his friend Reggie Love, a former college basketball star.

Hundreds of questions were hurled at him as Election Day 2008 approached. Questions like: Do you have what it takes to run a country? Are you experienced enough? And, finally, the question that burned in the minds of so many people watching this contest from around the world:

Could a black man really win enough votes to occupy the White House?

CHAPTER SEVENTEEN

'Change has come to America!'

Back in 1968, presidential nominee Robert Kennedy, brother of the late US President, John F. Kennedy, predicted: 'Things are moving so fast in race relations. A negro could be President in forty years.' One week later he was shot and killed.

Forty years later, on 4 November 2008, more than 130 million Americans went to the polls. It was the largest turnout of voters in United States history. People began lining up even before the polling stations opened to make sure they were part of the historic event. Some people were in the queue as early as 4.30 a.m. Some had not slept at all the night before.

Among the voters were Barack and Michelle Obama. They took Malia and Sasha with them to their neighbourhood polling station in Chicago.

Having returned from a final campaign event the night before, Barack did what he usually does before a big day in his political life. He played basketball. Twice in his contest with Hillary Clinton he had skipped his practice, and on the day the ballots were cast, he had lost. He was not taking any chances this time! For two hours he played on a basketball court near his home and tried to focus on something beside the election.

He thought, too, of his beloved grandmother, Toot. Two days before Election Day, she had passed away in Hawaii, but not before Obama had suspended his campaign and visited her one last time, and not before she had voted for her beloved grandson as he ran the race of his life.

The race was on. Over two million people used the absentee ballot, which allowed them to vote by mail or Internet. Americans everywhere expressed excitement and pride in their country after they had voted. Many people had done so for the first time in their lives. At the same time, in an effort to sabotage the system, anonymous emails were sent to young voters across the nation stating falsely that Election Day was postponed to the following day. No one knows how many people believed that message and did not vote as a result.

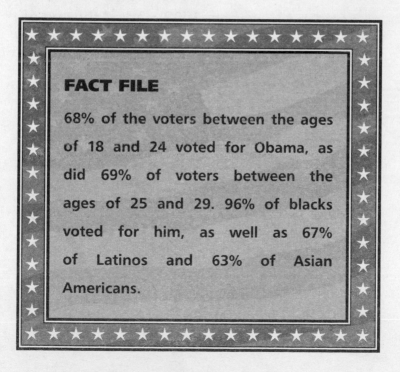

FACT FILE

68% of the voters between the ages of 18 and 24 voted for Obama, as did 69% of voters between the ages of 25 and 29. 96% of blacks voted for him, as well as 67% of Latinos and 63% of Asian Americans.

Thousands of people started to gather at Grant Park in Chicago even before the winner of the election was declared. Among the celebrities present was Oprah Winfrey, who had supported Obama from the beginning of his campaign.

Ohio was the last state that was needed to put Obama ahead of his opponent. When the result came in shortly before 11.00 p.m., 125,000 people cheered. It was deafening!

Tuesday 4 November 2008 marked the end of the longest presidential campaign season in the history of the United States. It was twenty-one months long. When all the votes were counted, there was no doubt that Barack Obama had won.

A country with a history of slavery and segregation had shocked the world by electing the son of an African to the most powerful office in the world.

John McCain graciously congratulated Obama for his victory and told supporters, 'This is a historic election, and I recognize the significance it has for African Americans and for the special

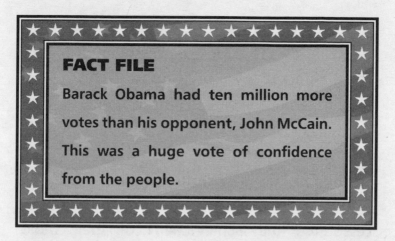

FACT FILE

Barack Obama had ten million more votes than his opponent, John McCain. This was a huge vote of confidence from the people.

pride that must be theirs tonight.' He added, 'We both realize that we have come a long way from the injustices that once stained our nation's reputation.'

'Wow!' exclaimed Obama, as he gulped down some water before he addressed the screaming crowd in Grant Park with the following historic statement:

'If there is anyone out there who still doubts that America is a place where all things are possible, who still wonders if the dream of our founders is alive in our time, who still questions the power of our democracy, tonight is your answer . . . Change has come to America.'

The crowd went wild!

Hours after his victory, crowds continued to celebrate on the streets of Washington and in Obama's home town of Chicago, Illinois.

In his father's village in Kenya, people danced through the night with Granny Obama.

In Jakarta, Indonesia, his former classmates cheered for 'Curly Eyelashes'.

In Honolulu, students at Punahou School celebrated the achievement of their most famous graduate.

In the UK and Europe and all over the world, people celebrated the first person of colour to govern a country with a majority white population.

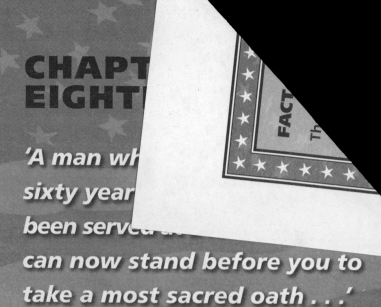

CHAPTER EIGHT

*'A man wh
sixty year
been serve
can now stand before you to
take a most sacred oath . . .'*

Before Barack Obama could be sworn into office he needed to form an administration to run the country. He had about two months to accomplish this task. After British general elections, the outgoing Prime Minister has to vacate the official Downing Street residence by lunchtime the following day, but in the USA the handover period is much longer.

The day Barack Obama took the Oath of Office was always going to be a very special

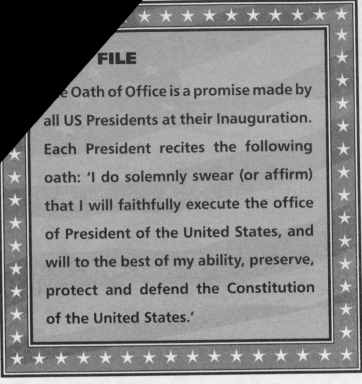

FILE

e Oath of Office is a promise made by all US Presidents at their Inauguration. Each President recites the following oath: 'I do solemnly swear (or affirm) that I will faithfully execute the office of President of the United States, and will to the best of my ability, preserve, protect and defend the Constitution of the United States.'

day. But it was even more special than anyone could ever have guessed.

Voters rarely seek to share the spotlight with a politician, but the Inauguration of Barack Hussein Obama was an extraordinary exception. Nearly two million people came to Washington on 20 January 2009 and flooded the grounds of the National Mall to participate in the swearing-in of the 44th President.

They came from every region of America and from countries around the world. In the crowds were grandparents and toddlers, housewives and businessmen, veterans wearing military honours, firefighters, schoolteachers, factory workers, farmers and a teenager with the word 'Obama' shaved on his head. They were eyewitnesses to an unparalleled moment in American history.

'It's amazing in the fact that everyone felt a common bond,' said a woman who had travelled from Florida to attend the event. 'We don't know each other but we feel—'

'– a oneness,' agreed another woman at her side, who had participated in the March on Washington in 1963 to protest segregation and racial bias in America. Her eleven-year-old grandson called the Inauguration 'amazing'.

Addressing the crowd, Obama said that his assumption of office symbolized 'who we are and how far we have travelled'. His election was made possible, he said, because the Americans had 'chosen hope over fear, unity of purpose over conflict and discord'. He extended a generous hand to the rest of the world, saying that America was a friend of 'every man, woman, and child who seeks a future of peace and dignity'.

The audience responded with gusto and the Mall was turned into a shimmering mass of red, white and blue as people waved miniature American flags.

Thanks to the global reach of modern communications, the eyes and ears of people around the world also heard his message. More than 100 million people outside the United States watched live broadcasts of Obama's swearing-in. They gathered in front of TV sets in libraries, pubs, factories, public plazas and homes. Countless others witnessed the event on the Internet.

In the Kenyan village where Obama's father was born, Luo tribesmen danced in his honour under a banner that read: CONGRATULATIONS TO OUR SON, OUR HOPE.

Widyanto Hendro, who once shared a desk with Obama at primary school in Indonesia, joined former classmates in Jakarta to celebrate the Inauguration. 'Who'd have thought it when we were messing around together in the second back row of the class,' he laughed.

A ceremonial bell was rung in the Japanese town that bears Obama's name, and in Donegal, Ireland, which claims to be the home of several of his mother's ancestors, a group sang in praise of O'Reilly, O'Leary, O'Sullivan, O'Hara . . . *'There's no one as Irish as Barack O'Bama.'*

After the celebration on the Mall, a parade took the new First Family to their living quarters, the White House. When Barack and Michelle stepped out of their limousine to greet wellwishers, the thrill of excitement among those who had waited hours for a glimpse of the new President was described as 'electric, like a spark arcing from a live wire'. The couple walked around for nearly ten minutes, then returned to their limousine to repeated chants of 'O-bam-a!' Throughout the day, the crowd was enormously disciplined. There were no reports of disturbances or unruly behaviour or even commonplace jostling.

That evening the Obamas participated in another tradition of American politics – a series of inaugural balls. Normally these are stuffy events open only to other politicians and campaign contributors who have paid the costs of the campaign.

But once more, Barack Obama broke with tradition. He and Michelle made their first appearance not at a banquet for the rich and famous, but at the Neighborhood Ball, a first-ever event to honour the people at the heart of his campaign, the neighbourhood organizers.

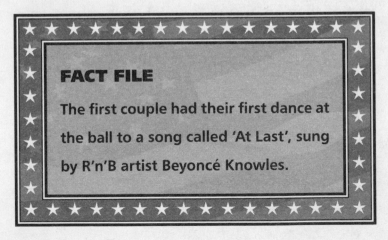

FACT FILE

The first couple had their first dance at the ball to a song called 'At Last', sung by R'n'B artist Beyoncé Knowles.

As he left, the new President told the crowd, 'Let's go change America,' and challenged them to return to their communities and work for the common good. He was echoing the message that he had delivered so forcefully in his inaugural speech a few hours earlier.

As their long day neared its end, Barack and Michelle attended the Commander-in-Chief's Ball. This event honoured American soldiers. It was held at the National Building Museum, a beautiful Washington landmark. They shared an inaugural dance with Vice President Biden and his wife, Jill.

One of the military men in attendance, Lieutenant Derrick Read, summed up the view of many Americans by saying, 'It definitely shows how far we've come in this country.' He then added, 'He's more than just a black President. He's the people's President, and I'm honoured to serve under him.'

Community organization, then Barack moves into political campaigning . . . and success!

The pressure is on!
Barack runs for President

. . . with support from
Granny Sarah in Kenya

. . . and a TV debate with the Republican candidate, John McCain

November 2008 – Election Night!

. . . and the new First Family celebrate victory!

An historic day – 20 January 2009 – as Barack Obama is sworn in as the 44th President of the USA

Despite near freezing winter weather, nearly 2 million people assemble in Washington DC...and 140 million people watch on TV around the world

Obama becomes President,
swearing the Oath on
Abraham Lincoln's Bible

A perfect day!

CHAPTER NINETEEN
The First 100 Days

'There are many who won't agree with every decision or policy I make as President, and we know that government can't solve every problem. But I will always be honest with you about the challenges we face. I will listen to you . . .'

By any measure, what Barack Obama has achieved in his first months in office is remarkable. He aimed high, with his pledge for 'change we can believe in', and he and his administration began to deliver exactly that. Worldwide there has been a major financial crisis, with many countries struggling to balance the books, so he has a very tough job ahead of him.

Opinion polls taken in these first few months showed that Americans approve of Barack Obama's leadership. A majority of people from both the Democratic and Republican parties said that Obama is trying to work in a 'bipartisan' way in order to solve difficult problems facing the country.

Here are some of the key moments in the first 100 days.

☆ Day 1 – 20 January 2009
Inauguration speech.

☆ Day 3
Signs an order to close Guantanamo Bay – an American military base in Cuba where suspected terrorists are held before trial.

☆ Day 7
Issues rules for more fuel-efficient cars and small lorries.

✫ Day 10

Signs a bill or draft law making it easier for employees to sue for work/pay discrimination.

✫ Day 16

Signs a bill extending health coverage to 4 million uninsured children, and raises the tax on tobacco.

Sets a limit on salaries and bonuses paid to company bosses who have received taxpayers' money to help them through the recent financial crisis.

✫ Day 19–20

The family spend the weekend in Camp David, used by Presidents' families for holidays for 50 years.

✫ Day 21

Trip to Elkhart County, Indiana, where unemployment is double the US average.

☆ **Day 22**

Nearly 37 million Americans watch President Obama's first prime-time press conference. This is over 6 million more viewers than for American Idol, which is the most watched TV show.

☆ **Day 28**

Introduces a bill that commits billions of dollars of government money to jumpstart the economy. It will create or save 3 million jobs.

☆ **Day 29**

Approves sending 17,000 more troops to Afghanistan.

☆ **Day 30**

Orders banks that had been given taxpayers' money by the government to reduce monthly mortgage payments for families facing the loss of their homes.

☆ **Day 31**

Meets with Michelle Jean, the first black Governor General of Canada.

☆ Day 36

Addresses Congress on his budget plan to spend government money on education, health, repairs to highways, sewers and other public works.

☆ Day 39

Addresses thousands of soldiers, to say: 'Let me say this as plainly as I can: by August 31 2010, our combat mission in Iraq will end.'

☆ Day 43

Gordon Brown, the British Prime Minister, visits the White House and praises Obama as a 'transformative' leader. Obama speaks of his mother's British ancestry and says the relationship between Britain and the US is 'not only special and strong, but one that will get stronger as time goes on'.

☆ Day 60

Tells Iran he wants to end differences between the two countries.

☆ Day 66

Answers the public's questions live online. 90,000 questions were submitted for the President to choose from.

☆ Day 72

President and Mrs Obama visit London to see the Prime Minister and many other heads of state. Jamie Oliver prepares the dinner for the world leaders and their guests (including *Harry Potter* author J.K. Rowling and athlete Dame Kelly Holmes).

☆ Day 73

Michelle Obama talks to students at the Elizabeth Garrett Anderson School for girls in Islington, north London. She gets a rapturous welcome and the event gets huge media coverage in the UK. Later, she meets patients at the Charing Cross Hospital with the Prime Minister's wife, Sarah Brown.

The Obamas meet the Queen of England.

☆ Day 76

The President makes a speech on nuclear disarmament from Prague Castle in the capital of the Czech Republic. Over 20,000 people come to hear him. The same day, North Korea launches a rocket into space. The rocket is believed by many governments, including the US, to be a threatening nuclear device. President Obama condemns this act.

☆ Day 77

Obama visits Turkey to speak about better relations between Muslim countries. 'We will listen carefully, bridge misunderstanding and seek common ground,' he promises.

☆ Day 78

Visits Iraq.

☆ Day 84

The Obamas host the Easter Egg Roll, an annual egg race and hunt on the White House lawn. This tradition dates back to 1878!

✯ Day 86

Honouring his promise to his two daughters, President Obama introduces a new puppy to the White House. Bo, a six-month-old Portuguese water dog, is an immediate hit.

✯ Day 87

Makes public information on harsh interrogation techniques regarded by many as torture, which the previous US government had authorized. President Obama condemns these actions as illegal and not to be allowed in future.

✯ Day 93

Earth Day: President Obama announces a move to generate more wind and wave renewable energy. This move will help the environment for years to come.

✯ Day 94

The President meets credit card company bosses to tell them to stop raising prices unfairly.
Take Your Child to Work Day: Michelle Obama hosts the children of White House staff.

☆ **Day 98**

Obama makes an emergency speech about the spreading swine flu disease.

☆ **Day 99**

An important member of the Republican Party changes sides to join Obama.

☆ **Day 100**

Obama reports back to the world on the decisions and actions he has taken during his first 100 days in office.

CHAPTER TWENTY

A Typical Day in the White House

'Greatness is never a given. It must be earned.'

According to aides, Barack Obama gets to the Oval Office, the President's formal workspace in the White House, a little after 8.00 a.m. and works until about 1.00 a.m. the following day.

His typical morning is divided up into back-to-back briefings with different teams working on specific issues like national security or economics, followed by meetings with his staff, members of his Cabinet and other department heads. Between meetings, he talks to international leaders and confers with governors and members of Congress.

Obama usually holds a public event at about 11.00 a.m. and then eats lunch in the Oval Office with a senior official, including a weekly lunch with Vice President Biden.

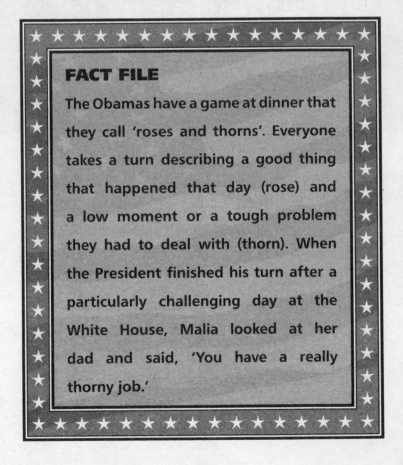

FACT FILE

The Obamas have a game at dinner that they call 'roses and thorns'. Everyone takes a turn describing a good thing that happened that day (rose) and a low moment or a tough problem they had to deal with (thorn). When the President finished his turn after a particularly challenging day at the White House, Malia looked at her dad and said, 'You have a really thorny job.'

He prefers to move around in the afternoons when possible and leaves the White House to visit Cabinet members and government departments. 'Barack is determined not to be engulfed in "the bubble",' said Eleanor Holmes Norton, a longtime friend, referring to the closed and isolated world of aides and official events that surrounded the former President Bush.

One way to break free from 'the bubble' is the enjoyable time he spends with his family. Dinner with Michelle, Malia and Sasha is a very important part of his day.

During the presidential campaign, Obama promised voters that he would travel outside the capital for regular doses of 'reality'. In his first month in office, he visited five states to discuss his economic recovery plan with voters. He made additional trips to discuss foreign policy and other issues. This amounted to more travel outside of Washington in the first month in office than any of the previous five presidents.

And there is one more way in which this

remarkable man keeps grounded. Every morning his staff delivers him a package of ten letters that were mailed to the White House. The letters may contain advice by a businessman in California or a plea for help from a welfare mother in Buffalo. In between his daily meetings with powerful heads of state and leaders in Washington, Barack sits alone behind his desk and reads the letters, one at a time. Thus, the boy who was born to a teenage mother on the far periphery of the US, some 5,000 miles from the Oval Office, can stay connected with the hopes and dreams and struggles of everyday Americans.

His dream had become reality!

'All are equal,
all are free,
and all deserve
a chance to pursue
their full measure
of happiness.'

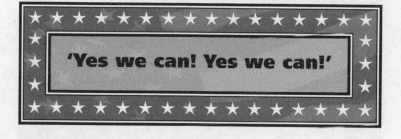

'Yes we can! Yes we can!'

FACT FILE
ON THE PRESIDENT

Over 52% of voters chose Obama in the election – that's nearly 70 million people!

There are over 300 million Americans. Barack Obama's title is Commander-in-Chief. He is the head of the army and navy; and of all the US citizens.

As US President, Barack Obama travels in special transport. Air Force 1, a private jet, is kitted out with three floors, a meeting room, an office and an operating room in case the President feels unwell. The President's black limousine is nearly six metres long and two metres high, with thick armour-plating all round. The tyres are a massive 50 centimetres high, the sort usually found on commercial trucks.

The White House has 132 rooms on six floors. There is a cinema, a tennis court, a swimming pool, a running track and a bowling alley. (It was rumoured that Obama might prefer to have a basketball court!) The room where the President works is called the Oval Office. The five professional chefs in the kitchens can serve up to 1,000 guests.

FACT FILE
ON THE US POLITICAL SYSTEM

Congress is where American laws are discussed and changed, and new laws (called bills) are written. The bills are then sent to the President to sign if he or she agrees with them.

If the President does not agree with a bill, it cannot become the law unless two-thirds of the people in Congress support it. This is the only way that they can overrule the President.

Congress is made up of two groups: the House of Representatives and the Senate. Both houses make decisions by voting. Both groups meet in the Capitol building, which is shown on the front of this book.

Every politician in Congress is elected by the people in one of the 50 states.

Congress is like the British Parliament, which is also made up of two groups: the House of Lords and the House of Commons.

Five facts about the House of Representatives

1. Each state receives representation in the House in proportion to its population, so the state with the most people – California – has the most representatives.

2. The House has the power to choose the President if neither of the presidential candidates win most of the people's votes.

3. The person in charge of the House is called the 'speaker'.

4. You have to be 25 years old to be a representative.

5. Each representative keeps the job for two years, and then there is another election.

Five facts about the Senate

1. The Senate has just two people representing each state. Because America has 50 states, there are always 100 politicians in the Senate.

2. The 100 senators cannot design laws that would raise taxes or create new taxes on the people.

3. A senator's speech can last as long as they want! But they are not allowed to make more than two speeches on the same law in one day.

4. The Vice President – Obama's second-in-command, Joe Biden – is the head of the Senate. If there is a tie in the number of votes, he has the final deciding vote.

5. You have to be 30 years old to be a senator, and you keep the job for six years.

THE FIGHT FOR EQUALITY

'I am the son of a black man from Kenya and a white woman from Kansas . . . I've gone to some of the best schools in America and lived in one of the poorest nations. I am married to a black American who carries within the blood of slaves and slave owners – an inheritance we pass on to our two precious daughters . . .'

So much has changed for the better since Barack Obama's father, Barack Sr, first arrived in Hawaii in 1959. Here are some of the key moments in the fight for equal rights and opportunities from this period onwards, not only in the USA, but also in the UK and elsewhere.

★ **1954:** The segregation of schools is declared illegal in the USA.

★ **1955:** In Alabama – a southern state in the USA – Rosa Parks refuses to give up her seat on a bus to a white man. Dr Martin Luther King organizes the Birmingham Bus Boycott, sparking the civil rights movement.

★ **1957:** Nine black students try to attend a newly mixed school in Little Rock, in the south of America. They have to be protected from a mob of protesters by police and soldiers. Only one of them manages to graduate.

☆ **1960:** Black students in the US begin peaceful protests, 'sit-ins', by sitting in the cafeteria at Woolworths, even though only white customers were allowed seats. This leads to a mixed cafeteria later that year.

☆ **1963:** Dr Martin Luther King gives his famous 'I Have a Dream' speech to over 250,000 people gathered for a March on Washington for Jobs and Freedom.

☆ **1964:** The Civil Rights Act becomes law in the US. It authorizes equal access to public facilities and bans discrimination in employment and education.

☆ **1965:** The US Voting Rights Act bans anyone from denying black people the right to vote.

☆ **1965:** The Race Relations Act is passed in the UK. This makes open discrimination on the grounds of race illegal.

✯ **1968**: Dr Martin Luther King is assassinated in the USA.

✯ **1972**: Shirley Chisholm, a black female politician and educator, runs for President of the United States, 'in spite of hopeless odds . . . to demonstrate the sheer will and refusal to accept the status quo'.

✯ **1976**: The Commission for Racial Equality is founded in the UK.

✯ **1984**: Civil rights activist Reverend Jesse Jackson – a black leader – runs for President; he also runs in 1988.

✯ **1990**: Apartheid ends in South Africa. Nelson Mandela, the anti-apartheid activist, is freed from prison after 27 years.

✯ **1991**: Rodney King, a 25-year-old African American, is videotaped being beaten by several police officers in Los Angeles. The incident brings to light issues of police brutality towards black people and leads to a riot in the city.

⭐ **1993:** Carol Moseley Brown becomes the first and only black woman elected to the US Senate. She runs for President in 2004.

⭐ **1993:** In south London, black student Stephen Lawrence, aged 18, is murdered on his way home. Although five white men are arrested as suspects of the unprovoked attack, nobody has been jailed. Stephen's parents campaign for justice and in 1999 a government report on the police service finds that it is deeply racist. Changes are made.

⭐ **1997:** Kofi Annan becomes the first black head of the United Nations.

⭐ **1998:** The Human Rights Act is passed in the UK. It adds to the European Convention on Human Rights and ensures that anyone who is in the UK for any reason has fundamental human rights which government and public authorities must respect. This includes laws against discrimination.

⭐ **2001:** Colin Powell becomes the US Secretary of State, the highest-ranking US government post held by an African American.

⭐ **2008:** Barack Obama is elected as the first black President of the United States.

FURTHER READING

For more on Barack Obama, his official website is the best place to start:

www.barackobama.com

You can also visit the White House website at:

www.whitehouse.gov

For more resources on black history:

www.blackhistorymonthuk.co.uk

For more about politics or a career in politics (in the UK):

www.headsup.org.uk

www.direct.gov.uk/en/YoungPeople/

DG_10016203

For more information about your personal rights:

www.equalityhumanrights.com

The Equality and Human Rights Commission in Britain was formed in October 2007, and builds on the legacies of the Equal Opportunities Commission, the Commission for Racial Equality and the Disability Rights Commission to work towards the elimination of all discrimination, reduce inequality, protect human rights and build good relations, ensuring that everyone has a fair chance in life.

BIBLIOGRAPHY

Books

Dougherty, Steve. *Hopes and Dreams: The Story of Barack Obama*. New York: Black Dog & Leventhal, 2008

Mendell, David. *Obama: From Promise to Power*. New York: HarperCollins, 2007; UK: Canongate Books, 2007

Obama, Barack. *Dreams from My Father: A Story of Race and Inheritance*. New York: Random House, 1995, 2004; UK: Canongate Books, 2007

Obama, Barack. *The Audacity of Hope: Thoughts on Reclaiming the American Dream*. New York: Crown, 2006

Olive, David (ed.). *An American Story: The Speeches of Barack Obama*. Toronto, Canada: ECW Press, 2008

Staff of *The New York Times*. *Obama: The Historic Journey*. New York: Callaway, 2009

Thomas, Garen. *Yes We Can: A Biography of Barack Obama*. New York: Feiwel and Friends, 2008

Articles (listed by date of publication)

'First Black Elected to Head Harvard's *Law Review*.' *New York Times*, 6 February 1990

'A Life's Calling to Public Service.' *Punahou Bulletin*, Autumn 1999

'The Candidate: How the Son of a Kenyan Economist Became an Illinois Everyman.' *New Yorker*, 31 May 2004

'The Legend of Barack Obama.' *Washingtonian*, 1 November 2006

'The Not-So-Simple Story of Barack Obama's Youth.' *Chicago Tribune*, 25 March 2007

'Barack Obama: Mother Not Just a Girl from Kansas.' *Chicago Tribune*, 27 March 2007

'A Kid Called Barry.' *Punahou Bulletin*, Spring 2007

'Obama Clinches Nomination, First Black Candidate to Lead a Major Party Ticket.' *New York Times*, 4 June 2008

'Though Obama Had to Leave to Find Himself, It Is Hawaii That Made His Race Possible.' *Washington Post*, 24 August 2008

'How Obama Writes His Speeches.' *Time*, 28 August 2008

'When Michelle Met Barack.' *Washington Post*, 5 October 2008

'Obama Elected President as Racial Barrier Falls.' *New York Times*, 4 November 2008

'Obama, Spider-Man on the Same Comic-Book Page.' *USA Today*, 9 January 2009

'Oratory Captures Nation's Mood.' *Baltimore Sun*, 18 January 2009

'Obama Inauguration: World Reaction.' *Financial Times*, 20 January 2009

'A Historic Inauguration Draws Throngs to the Mall.' *Washington Post*, 21 January 2009

'Poll Shows Broad Support for Obama Leadership.' *New York Times*, 24 February 2009

'Obama Gives Troops Timeline for Iraq War's End.' *Wall Street Journal*, 28 February 2009

'Obama, Reaching Outside the Bubble.' *Washington Post*, 1 March 2009

QUOTATIONS FROM SPEECHES BY BARACK OBAMA

Prologue

'No dream is beyond our grasp': *Wisconsin primary, 12 February 2008*

'I was not born into money or status': *Wisconsin primary, 12 February 2008*

'I think it is fair to say': *US Senate on the occasion of Rosa Parks' death, 25 October 2005*

Chapter One

'I was not born into money or status': *as above*

Chapter Two

'I know what it means to have an absent father': *Father's Day speech, Chicago, 15 June 2008*

Chapter Three

'Our patchwork heritage is a strength, not a weakness': *Inaugural address 20 January 2009*

Chapter Ten

'I'll never forget that my journey began on the streets of Chicago': *Iowa Caucus Night, 3 January 2008*

'If there is a child on the South Side of Chicago who can't read': *Democratic National Convention, 2004*

'I learned that meaningful change': *Video statement to supporters, 2007*

Chapter Eleven

'I feel comfortable in my own skin' *Rolling Stone magazine; interview*

Chapter Twelve

'For every one of me': *New York Times article, 6 February 1990*

'The fact that I've been elected': *New York Times as above*

Chapter Thirteen

'The rock of our family': *Election night speech, Chicago, 4 November 2008*

Chapter Fourteen

'There are some people who won't vote for me
    because I'm black': *US News and World Report*

'We have shared values': *New Yorker profile*

Chapter Fifteen

'To be the only African American':
    www.barackobama.com

'Got a scholarship' (and other extracts): *Democratic
    National Convention, 2004*

Chapter Sixteen

'The decision to run for President': *Ebony
    magazine; interview*

'All of us know what those challenges are today':
    *announcing candidacy, Illinois, 10 February
    2007*

'When we have faced impossible odds':
    *announcing candidacy, Illinois, 10 February
    2007*

Chapter Seventeen

'Change has come to America!' *Election night
    speech, 4 November 2008*

'If there is anyone out there who still doubts'
    Election night speech, 4 November 2008
'This is a historic election' [John McCain]: *Election
    night speech, 4 November 2008*

Chapter Eighteen

'A man whose father less than sixty years ago':
    Inaugural address, 20 January 2009
'Chosen hope over fear, unity of purpose over
    conflict and discord' *Inaugural address,
    20 January 2009*

Chapter Nineteen

'There are many who won't agree': *Election night
    speech, 4 November 2008*
'Let me say this': *Camp Lejeune, 27 February 2009*
'Not only special': *White House press conference,
    3 March 2009*
'We will listen carefully': *Turkish Assembly,
    6 April 2009*

Chapter Twenty

'Greatness is never a given': *Inaugural address,
    20 January 2009*

End pages

'All are equal, all are free': *Inaugural address,
20 January 2009*

'I am the son of a black man from Kenya':*speech
in Philadephia, 18 March 2008*

Permissions

For all acknowledgements and credits, every effort has been made to trace copyright holders and to credit quotations and sources accurately; but should there be any omissions or corrections needed, the publishers will be happy to correct for subsequent reprints.

Picture credits

With thanks for the permission to reproduce the photos as follows:

Cover images

Front cover: Getty Images (Obama waving)
Back cover: Mark Wilson/UPI/eyevine: (Inauguration); Alex Wong/Getty Images (with Bo, the dog); Polaris/eyevine (young Obama); Polaris/eyevine (with father); UPI/eyevine (with mother)

Inside colour section 1

i: AP/Press Association Images (*Barack Obama senior*); UPI/eyevine (*with mother*)
ii: Polaris/eyevine
iii: UPI/eyevine (*with family*); AP/Press Association Images (*school picture*)
iv: Polaris/eyevine (*both pictures*)
v: UPI/eyevine
vi: UPI/eyevine
vii: Polaris/eyevine (with grandmother); Toby Selander/ Polaris/eyevine (family group)
viii: Steve Liss/Polaris/eyevine

Inside colour section 2

i: Polaris/eyevine (*campaigning*); M. Spencer Green/ AP/Press Association Images (*with family*)

ii-iii: Charles Ommanney/Getty Images (*stadium picture*); Ben Curtis/AP/Press Association Images (*grandmother in Kenya*); Charles Ommanney/Getty Images (*TV debate*)

iv-v: Alex Brandon/AP/Press Association Images (*Election Night*); Jae C. Hong/AP/Press Association Images (*First Family*)

vi: Scott Andrews/UPI/eyevine (*crowds at the Capitol, top*); Mark Ralston/Getty Images (*supporter, centre*); Marvi Lacar/Getty Images (*crowd, foot*)

viii: Win McNamee/UPI/eyevine (*crowd, top*)

vii: Mark Wilson/UPI/eyevine (*taking the Oath, foot*); Robyn Beck/Getty Images (*Mall walk*); Saul Loeb/ Getty Images (*first couple dancing*); Getty Images (*Obama waving*)

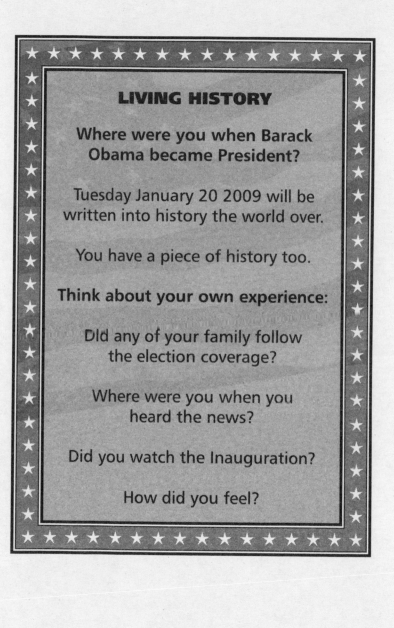

LIVING HISTORY

Where were you when Barack Obama became President?

Tuesday January 20 2009 will be written into history the world over.

You have a piece of history too.

Think about your own experience:

Did any of your family follow the election coverage?

Where were you when you heard the news?

Did you watch the Inauguration?

How did you feel?

About the Author

'When the news came, I was curled up in bed under the covers with my fingers stuck in my ears. I was too nervous and excited to watch the television. The moment he won, I heard this ear-splitting scream. Then I realized it was coming from me . . . '

Dawne Allette lives in Baltimore, USA. She was born in Grenada, a Caribbean island, and has lived in Britain and Iran. Dawne is a journalist for the *Baltimore Times* newspaper, and a creative writing teacher. She also works on a literacy programme for Baltimore Public Schools.

Dawne has written a number of children's picture books that are noted for their inspiration, lyricism and humour.

Other biographies available from Tamarind for younger readers

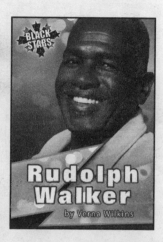

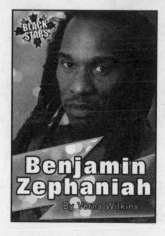

To see the rest of our list, please visit our website:

www.**tamarindbooks**.co.uk

Other Tamarind titles
for junior readers

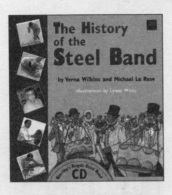

To see the rest of our list, please visit our website:

www.**tamarindbooks**.co.uk